THE LOCAL STATE
Public Money and American Cities

STANFORD STUDIES IN THE NEW POLITICAL HISTORY

Allan Bogue, David W. Brady, Nelson W. Polsby, and
Joel H. Silbey, Editors

The Local State

Public Money and American Cities

ERIC H. MONKKONEN

STANFORD UNIVERSITY PRESS
Stanford, California   1995

Stanford University Press
Stanford, California

© 1995 by the Board of Trustees of the
Leland Stanford Junior University

Printed in the United States of America

CIP data appear at the end of the book

Stanford University Press publications are
distributed exclusively by Stanford University Press
within the United States, Canada, Mexico, and Central
America; they are distributed exclusively by Cambridge
University Press throughout the rest of the world.

Acknowledgments

For supporting the research reported in Chapter 2, I wish to thank the Academic Senate of the University of California, Los Angeles. I also wish to thank two able, long-suffering research assistants, Jacqueline Braitman and Miriam Meijer, for scanning local newspapers and digging up obscure citations. The hunt for specific legal information could not have been accomplished without the aid of three other research assistants, Amelia Kremer, Benjamin Keppel, and Thomas Clark. In addition, the interlibrary loan staff at UCLA's University Research Library deserves special thanks for finding the hundreds of local newspapers searched during the course of this project.

For the work in Chapters 3 and 4, I wish to acknowledge the assistance of Laura J. Berk and George Heerman of the Illinois State Historical Library; Cullom Davis of Sangamon State College; and John Hoffman of the Illinois Historical Survey. The comments and thoughts of Frank Munger of the SUNY Buffalo Law School; Stephen Diamond of the University of Miami Law School; Steve Daniels of the American Bar Foundation; Robin Einhorn of the University of California, Berkeley; John Majewski of UCLA; Terrence McDonald of the University of Michigan; John Brown of Clark University; and my colleagues Bruce Schulman and Gary Schwartz have made these chapters better.

I am convinced that historians must direct their research based on the implications of their questions, not simply on what the past hands us as the big events. To follow such a research program can mean that the needle in the haystack must be tracked, and the dog that did not bark must be investigated assiduously. My effort to do just that has been facilitated most by a grant from the Law and Social Science Program of the National Science Foundation, Social and Economic Sciences 87 10230, splendidly administered by the staff of UCLA's Institute for Social Science Research.

Contents

Tables and Figures

Tables

Figures

THE LOCAL STATE
Public Money and American Cities

The Importance of
Local Finance

WITH THE UNITED STATES on the way to becoming an almost completely urban nation, the financing of cities has become an issue of great urgency. Put simply, American cities do not have enough money. But to say much more than this makes the issue very complex. The problems (and solutions) branch in two directions, by revenues and by expenditures. If a shortage of the former is the source of the problem, then there is some sort of tax dysfunction. If the latter are the problem, then there is unacceptable spending. To make things even more complex, revenues and expenditures happen in real time, politically speaking — if the city does not actually collect some money, it has none to spend. Like other economic actors, the city manipulates the time dimension by borrowing. It borrows in two ways: for the short term (less than a year) to get over time gaps in revenue flows, and for the long term when the amount of money is so large that it cannot be repaid quickly. It is the long-term debt that funds the building of cities. It pays for the big stage on which the city's social, economic, and cultural life are all played out. Long-term debt funds the streets, buildings, and sewers: it is literally the foundation of modern urban life.

City finance is, moreover, an aspect of "political economics," for the shaping and operating of cities has required internal political adroitness in addition to a healthy economic system. This point has been very difficult for urbanists to assert, for politicians and the media often portray fiscal crises in cities as externally caused. In a recent book examining the current fiscal status of Chicago and New

York, Ester R. Fuchs has demonstrated how politics has made a major difference in the fiscal health of these two cities. She argues that the Democratic party's political machine actually preserved Chicago from the fiscal crises that have plagued machineless New York City. Other urban political scientists, among them Terry N. Clark, Paul Peterson, Ira Katznelson, and Martin Shefter, have made similar points, but Fuchs pushes the argument for the significance of political parties even farther than they do.

There is a growing body of work by people in several disciplines that is helping us reconceptualize cities as the extraordinarily complex political, cultural, social, geographical, and economic creatures they have become. I have profited enormously from the work of these and other urban scholars. In this body of relatively new literature, there are many disagreements and lacunae. Some disagreements are fundamental — for example, on the role of the world economy (Feagin 1988) versus the role of the mayor (Fuchs 1992).[1] And some lacunae also distort: almost all of the major research has been on very large cities, even though most urbanites live in smaller cities and clearly demonstrate their continued preference for them.

This book is about American cities in general, but it draws most of its examples from among the smaller, less well known ones. I have used these smaller cities for several reasons. To begin with, a large proportion of urbanites live in them. As Figure 1 shows, only from 1910 to 1950 did more people live in cities with over 100,000 inhabitants than in cities and towns with between 2,500 and 99,999. Considered as individual places, big cities have more clout — hence the attention they get — but from the point of view of people living in cities, more are in small places. (Many would probably argue, too, that 100,000 people — the population of present-day Springfield, Illinois, for instance — do not constitute a "big" city.) In any case, from the legal point of view, each city is an individual corporate entity, and what's law for the goose is (usually) law for the gander. As it happens, one of the best-known rulings about cities, even today, is an 1863 decision of the Iowa Supreme Court about Dubuque, at the time a city of under 15,000 people. Probably because the little-known justice who wrote the decision also wrote a

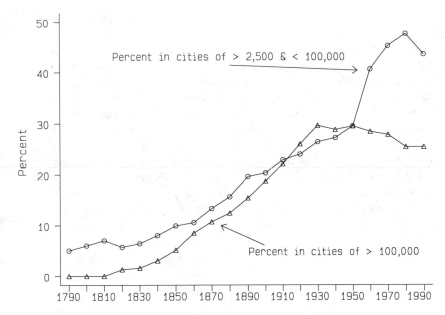

Figure 1. Percentage of total U.S. population in cities and towns with population greater than 2,500 and 100,000, 1790–1990. Sources: Calculated from *Historical Statistics of the United States, Colonial Times to 1970, Bicentennial Edition* (Washington, D.C.: USGPO, 1975) and *Statistical Abstract of the United States* (Washington, D.C.: USGPO, various dates).

(*the* nineteenth-century) textbook on municipal law, tiny Dubuque figures in one of the most Gothamized of recent urban histories.[2]

What I believe the research reported in this book shows is that "political" has a significance that goes beyond parties, and that the nuances and scope of political activity must be examined with an eye to surprise and contradiction. Too often, for instance, law gets separated from the political realm, and we forget that laws come from legislatures. Too often court decisions get misinterpreted as "pro" or "anti" when that is not at all the case. And too often we view political actors as either more or less creative than they actually are.

The central sections of this book analyze Illinois, not because it contains Chicago, but because by reason of its intensive development after the mid nineteenth century and its mix of small towns and mid-sized cities—of agricultural-processing, extractive, and industrial sites—its experiences exemplify those of the urban industrial North, which so powered American urbanization. For a century, however, Illinois's 1870 constitution limited the borrowing abilities of its cities, and it has been assumed that this caused local politicians to invent entirely new, undemocratic forms of government in order to avoid those limits. For example, in a conclusion based on a 1907 article by municipal reformer and political scientist Charles Merriam, historian Thomas C. Pegram asserts that "constitutional limits on the city's [Chicago's] bonded indebtedness further sapped its financial strength" (Pegram 1992, 94). Cities could not borrow over 5 percent of their assessed property value, so they encouraged the creation of separate fiscal authorities that do not resemble cities, towns, or any other sort of municipal entity.

Today, the mayor and city council of any American city are merely the most visible elements in an accretion of authorities, special districts, agencies, commissions, and boards. Sometimes these entities are unencumbered and powerful; more typically, their directorships overlap with the city council, a local political party, or other powerful local interest groups. They seldom have elected directors, and their policies are seldom included when public policy is debated. From port districts to transport authorities, from forest preserves to housing authorities, these various special agencies can borrow beyond constitutional limits. Because their ability to repay these "revenue bonds" is tied to secure revenues—either fees or taxes directly generated by specific new projects—they are excellent risks. Because they are governed by appointees, they seem more responsible. They form a thick structure of organized fiscal power, but few analysts consider them when analyzing city government.

If the governance by special districts was only a way of avoiding constitutionally imposed debt limitation, then such districts should no longer have been necessary after Illinois's new 1970 constitution removed such limits. Instead, they are still being created; to cite only one example, the Illinois Sports Facilities Authority, created in 1987, has built and operates a sports stadium in Chicago (Fuchs 1992). Clearly, if new authorities continued to be created after the constitutional limits on cities were eased, one must conclude that they were not invented solely to evade a constitution.

Urban politicians have been bending rules and creating new ones probably from time immemorial — certainly, as shown here, since the mid nineteenth century. Current organizational devices — call them nontraditional local governments — thus continue a long and constantly reelaborated tradition. There is no single key to find, no one hidden structure to expose.[3] That is why the topic is so interesting, and why scholarly disagreements multiply and evolve almost faster than the cities studied.

Like many city dwellers of the late twentieth century, I had long thought that the city was the political poor stepchild of the American polity. The famous headline "[President] Ford to City: Drop Dead" expressed my understanding of the system. It seemed to capture the arrogance of public officials, while suggesting a larger political attitude toward cities that was cruel and exploitative. This rather vague understanding accompanied my sense that the suburbs had unfairly drained the deserving central city of its resources. The origins of this sorry state seemed to stretch back to the 1870s, when a judge named John Dillon wrote a legal treatise condemning U.S. cities to perpetual dependency on state governments. State governments, in turn, had a long history of putting over stingy constitutional rules on cities that reinforced this artificial subservience.

The research of many urban historians began to pull the props from under this scenario. The legal historian Jon Teaford claimed that state legislative committees on cities were actually dominated by representatives of the urban areas. Suburban history, triggered by Kenneth Jackson, began to give suburban cities a preeminence that the "sub" in suburban had concealed. The work of many social historians stressed over and over again that migrants to U.S. cities bought houses, thus directly entering the local tax economy. My own work on crime and police reminded me again and again that police were a local, not state or national, innovation, and that one stumbling block in their local history was always cost. Political scientists, sociologists, and historians working on the problems of American state formation, by not addressing the city, indirectly also piqued my curiosity. And my own attempt at a synthesis of city history, *America Becomes Urban*, made me attend more carefully to the nature of the U.S. city as a corporate entity in a political situation very different from those of cities in most other nations. I became convinced that the story of the U.S. city was in fact the story of thousands of these corporate entities, and that they were in aggregate very different from my inherited picture. For one thing, they were active, not just reactive. As corporate entities, they could take rather grand economic actions. But they were also political entities, whose actions were the outcome of internal political contests and debates. When thousands of these internal contests resulted in action all across the urban landscape, it was akin to the consensual action of thousands of individuals in a political arena.

The challenge I faced was how to figure out more precisely what these cities did, and how they used their legal and political structures. In spite of their autonomy, the activities of U.S. cities are similar. Just as they copy their predecessors, they copy each other. Perhaps because they have so much freedom, the risks are too great to do other than make small, incremental modifications when they act. In any case, from a historical perspective they look so much the same that restoring individuality becomes as important as finding fundamental patterns.

To do so, this book moves from the broad to the small, tracing in the first two chapters what appear to be the bigger issues and measures of local fiscal politics. The evidence in both chapters pointed me toward even more specific questions about local politics and political-economic behavior, so I focus in Chapters 3 and 4 on constitutional revisions in Illinois that limited the economic activities of cities and towns. Some of these activities led to court cases, making it possible, in Chapter 5, to move the whole story back to the national level, inasmuch as the U.S. Supreme Court became the final arbiter in local affairs.

And it is here that the concrete aspect of our federal system is to be found: cities have precise limits as to what they can and cannot do, but these limits often give them a way to escape obligation as much as they frustrate action. I conclude this study convinced that U.S. cities encompass the logic of the democratic state: they must persuade their inhabitants to tax themselves to support the political and built infrastructure. To do so they must constantly reestablish their credibility and legitimacy, must constantly renegotiate their share of taxpayers' money, and must constantly convince taxpayers that the borrowing and spending the city embarks on will ensure a decent present and a just future.

CHAPTER ONE

The Importance of the Local State and Its Fiscal Politics

> The true policy of every State, county or city is to aid, by liberal laws, anything that will tend to build up the same, and develop its resources. While avoiding the ruinous excesses to which Wisconsin, Minnesota, and other States, have run, we must avoid for ourselves a penny-wise policy which would drive all public works of magnitude from our borders.
>
> — *Rockford Gazette*, February 17, 1870
> (Illinois Historical Survey, "Cole Notes")

 IN THE 1830S AND 1840S, many state governments went through periods of fiscal cleansing, legislators and voters trimming and sometimes eliminating state debt. States slowly paid down their debt so that by the time of the Civil War, some were virtually debt free. As small towns and cities grew, they often began their corporate lives with fiscal restraints specific to their legal existence, usually statutory limits on taxes. Local governments therefore did not undergo the transformations that the states did, but because their tax limits, and occasional borrowing limits, were easily modified by specific legislation, they played a more and more important role in borrowing and spending. The second half of the nineteenth century saw local governments come under attack for their diffuse yet major role in the political economy. This attack has usually been depicted as one caused by local excess and corruption.

Thus, U.S. local urban finances of the nineteenth and early twentieth centuries are often depicted in two frames: (1) an era of profligate governments, wasteful expenditure, uncontrolled borrowing, and cozy deals with private business (Yearley 1970, 3–34), followed by (2) general revulsion and state government intervention. The capping of the profligacy of the first period began in the decades after the Civil War, when "public indignation" at "reckless" and "abandoned public borrowing" demanded state government vigilance and "safeguards" (Virtue 1949, 289, 305 at n. 68; Williams and Nehemkis 1937, 178; see also Keller 1977, 181–88). By 1881,

fifteen of the thirty-eight states of the Union had set ceilings on
local debt, and three more had authorized their legislatures to set
ceilings, most commonly at 5 percent of assessed valuation. Twenty-
four states had restricted the right of cities to invest in railways, and
twenty-five the right to own the stocks of private corporations (U.S.
Census Office 1884). A leading bond lawyer noted in 1912 that the
"best security of any bond purchaser is a *reasonable* limitation in the
authorized debt" (Reed 1912, 98; emphasis added). So rigorous
were these new controls that the history of local finance in the
twentieth century has been narrated as a tale of escape from unrea-
sonable control, an "emancipation" not completed until the "anni-
hilation of effective control" by revenue bonds after World War II
(Virtue 1949, 293).

This legislative transfer to state government of control of local
government debt would seem to have been a straightforward process, but it raises complex theoretical and historical problems. Usually we think of state control of local government from the internal
perspective of the local government: active state governments are
thought to go with passive local governments. In this study, however,
I conceptualize the local governments in question as highly political, vigorous, and quite varied actors themselves. Their fiscal behavior, in particular debt issuance, exemplifies how they actively used
their relatively new corporate borrowing privileges in private capital markets. The historical questions involve the reasons why state
constitutions or legislatures monitored local governments' fiscal
behavior. More broadly, the issues include the nature of all corporate fiscal behavior. What determined local government entrepreneurship? In an era that had been experimenting with government
entrepreneurship on both state and local levels, did externally mandated regulation irrationally constrict an emergent, local public/
private partnership? Did reactionary rural legislators stifle innovative locals?

Over the past two decades, from Massachusetts to California,
highly publicized referenda have sought to regulate local fiscal "excess" by limiting taxation. Recent survey research (see, e.g., Sears
and Citrin 1982) shows that such tax-limitation movements arise
from a visible suspicion of local and state government and a desire
for local control. They are restricted to neither the right nor the

left, and they employ the political tools of the Progressive Era—specifically, the popular initiative and the referendum. Moreover, there is historical precedent for interpreting tax limitation as progressive reform: the Illinois constitution of 1870, for example, was both fiscally restrictive and mandated universal male suffrage.

The statutory and constitutional limitation of local government debt thus remains an important interaction between government and popular political action, and analysis of the dimensions and processes of the early debt-limitation movement in the United States illuminates this now well established and virtually traditional process. As a basis for investigating legal control of local political economies by the regulatory movement (which usually conjures up the image of liberal reformers enacting legislation designed to curb the excesses of big business), Chapters 3 and 4 accordingly look at the making of the Illinois constitution of 1870, a previously unexamined state-level instance of fiscal limitation.

The building and behavior of the American state has become a subject high on the agendas of both theoretical and empirical research in political science and sociology. Stephen Skowronek (1982), for example, has reconceptualized the business regulatory movement of the late nineteenth century to characterize the nature of U.S. state making, an effort he finds to have been enfeebled by the decentralizing tendencies and tripartite division of the U.S. polity. Skowronek argues that in key areas, such as interstate commerce, regulators failed to exercise their legal mandate, unintentionally creating a weak federal government based on a diffuse response to external demands, which slowed the development of the American state. Skowronek has enlarged the way we think about the state, indirectly encouraging an inventive approach to conceptualizing state action, and his innovative work tying regulation to politics and state making constructs an explanatory paradigm of the developing American state. The research I report here challenges some aspects of Skowronek's analysis, inasmuch as individual states, not the national state, formed the core of American state building. While the local state was indeed limited, to see these limits as crippling has been a great, and long-lived, misperception. Moreover, any view of the American state and its regulatory mechanisms that does not include the local state in its framework is destined to be incomplete.

While Skowronek has concentrated on the federal level, and Theda Skocpol and Ray Gunn have focused more recently on state governments (Skocpol 1992; Gunn 1989), few theorists have incorporated the local state into their thinking. But U.S. historians have long understood that in our federal system, state building occurred at the local level. This study therefore looks at the local level, specifically the seemingly successful effort by the Illinois constitutional convention of 1870 to regulate the fiscal behavior of local governments.

The interface of law, corporate behavior, and democracy is the analytic problem: how does a law-making organization measure and control the unpredictable behavior of individual organizational actors that it has empowered? The problem is intertwined with the very nature of the American state, which has always been highly diffuse, the many state constitutions laying down the fundamental rules for prolific and varied local governments, which in turn have constituted the largest single sector of government. For example, in Illinois in 1869, small villages had the same debt load as the state government, counties twice the debt, and cities over six times the debt (calculated from Illinois 1870c, 100–105). Together, these little entities (even excluding Chicago) had far more fiscal wherewithal than did either the state or federal governments.

Local governments have shared their complex and ambiguous status with the business corporation, for both expanded in numbers and power throughout the second half of the nineteenth century. Unlike most economic actors, even other corporations, local governments have always presented troublesome control problems. Their semiautonomy, highly politicized nature, and fiscal independence separated them from the larger body politic that had created them and to which they contributed and belonged. Yet it is to them that we must turn to understand the activities, hence nature, of the American state. In describing the state and local political activities that restricted local fiscal capacity, yet simultaneously gave local governments increased room for maneuver, the empirical results presented in this book add new evidence to our understanding of the local state in America.

The underlying questions have to do with how legislative bodies, their constitutional rules, and the various mechanisms for implementing the rules govern the behavior of those most ambiguous of corporate entities, local governments. State constitutions made possible local governments' existence. But once created, local governments, like all political bodies, took on a life of their own. Their latent potential was enormous, yet often unrecognized. Should they be restrained? What could restrain them? In the late nineteenth century, the role of local governments changed dramatically: cities grew in number and size, and their modern services employed whole new bodies of workers. States faced the challenge of measuring local governmental behavior, which required conceptualizing it, even as that behavior changed. As nineteenth-century writers consistently stressed, local government was a creature of state government, but such assertions had little to do with actually observing and regulating the behavior of thousands of corporate actors doing complex and different things.

The period selected for this study is of critical importance for several reasons. At the end of the Civil War, as a consequence of their subvention of military recruitment, local governments in the North faced debts of a size never before contemplated. On the one hand, these debts demonstrated local governments' fiscal potential. The postwar era saw an enormous and creative expansion of the service activities of local governments, and their debt-issuing capacity helped in this expansion (Monkkonen 1988). On the other hand, however, this unanticipated expansion posed a challenge to their legal creators, state legislators, who must have known that they faced a real prospect of seeing state government shrink to minor insignificance relative to local government. Moreover, local government was often on the side of the other profligate corporations of the nineteenth century, the railroads, working closely with them to raise capital (Heckman 1988). This national situation was especially acute in Illinois, where the Illinois Central Railroad had been financed by a land grant from the federal government (Brownson 1915). Consequently, just as Illinois legislators moved to regulate the grain-storage industry directly (*Munn v. Illinois* [1877]), delegates to the constitutional convention worked to regulate local government directly. And the voters enthusiastically approved such regulation.

On the face of it, state government's limitation of local fiscal behavior seems too easily explained to merit investigation. For instance, one might conclude that the setting of uniform debt limits for all municipalities was a component of the growing aversion to a multitude of bills covering only one town or village at a time, hence the laying down of a general rule. It has only been the recent and rather accidental discovery of the wide variety, extent, and amount of local debt, and of the local impetus to limit local finances, that has called into question these theoretical exercises accounting for local fiscal behavior (McDonald 1986; Teaford 1984). Research on municipal defaults has raised additional questions, showing that with the exception of the Great Depression of the 1930s, politics rather than pure economic forces played a major role in local defaults (Monkkonen 1984). These results suggest that there has been a neat accounting for a triggering event that did not happen — that reform may not simply have responded to local irresponsibility. Given this discrepancy, the behavior of nineteenth-century local finance has become broadly problematic.[1] In short, we are obliged by the growth, range, and scope of local government's fiscal activities to reopen the question of the nature of the U.S. local government.

There are at least one class of legal explanation and one class of rational explanation that seem to account adequately for the limited power of municipal corporations, for the state limitation of municipal debt, and for the legislative and constitutional movements creating these limits in the post–Civil War era. The first concerns the law of corporate regulation; the second the idea that some issues are uniquely local, hence the province of local government. From both points of view, such limitations can be completely explained. However, in their customary form both fail to account for some of the seeming anomalies of local behavior, and here I wish to amend each.

The first relevant conceptual frame is that of the corporation and its regulation. The nineteenth century's "liberal" theory of the corporation stipulated that legislative charters had to enumerate explicitly what a corporation could not do, leaving what it *could* do open to the inventiveness of its directors. The same "liberal theory" applied to public corporations. Thus, while public corporations such as cities seem on paper to have had many limitations, these may have reduced their overall potential only a little.

Given the enormous borrowing potential granted to local governments, one might ask why so little, rather than so much, local debt was issued. I hypothesize that municipal corporations limited their own fiscal behavior, that state limitations were consensual, and that the main restriction on local fiscal behavior was by risk-averse voters rather than external controls. Reconceptualizing the issue of local debt and its control as a question of corporate behavior gives us a more appropriate analytic tool with which to begin investigating local government The mapping of local government's behavior is thereby shifted to a theoretical ground midway between the larger political system and the changing corporate environment: from this perspective, it is literally a political economy.

Regulation of economic processes is often considered either to be counterproductive (airline regulation), a confirmation and enforcement of the status quo (zoning), or a means of making stable an otherwise unstable environment (railroad regulation via the Interstate Commerce Commission). The latter two outcomes occur when the regulated "capture" regulators. In both of these cases, the argument is that economic actors prefer predictability to risk, choosing a stable — even if limited — market share, rather than one they might gain more from by competing in a riskier environment. In any case, the regulatory process is now considered to be more an aspect of governmental economic management than an arena of conflict, as it was thought to be during the Progressive Era. Viewed this way, the regulation of municipal behavior becomes a special case, just as municipalities are special kinds of corporations. Jon Teaford's important work has established that municipal interests were from early on represented on legislative committees — an early instance of regulatory capture (Teaford 1984). But as opposed to all other regulation, that of municipalities has special liabilities, for they contain voters, and partisan politics offers an improperly regulated municipality a means of redress. Hence, the regulation of municipalities, one of the earliest kinds of state regulation of corporations, provides an important paradigm for later regulatory behavior. At least three features of this thesis should be noted immediately: first, that apparent regulation may be used by the regulated in their own interests; second, and the obverse of the first, that we must be very cautious in interpreting the absence of regulatory actions; and third, that partisan stances may be purely symbolic and drained of any sensible rationale.

Local governments constitute a form of corporate entrepreneurship parallel to, but distinct from, the private sector. State constitutions have provided the legal architecture for this entrepreneurship. My argument is that constitutional restrictions should be viewed as clauses inserted in the enabling documents with the consent and participation of local governments. When only the enabling language is examined outside of its larger context, it seems to be highly restrictive. Consequently, modern proposals to change the nature of local governments identify state constitutions as simultaneously the empowering tools and the shackles by which local change can be effected or stifled (Fesler 1967, 570–71). Until recently, what is an untested hypothesis — that local government functions in a frustrating legal context imposed by state and federal fundamental law — has been an axiom dominating the political and legal analysis of U.S. cities. The research presented here on the post–Civil War fiscal and local political context of Illinois, a key state in the debt-limitation movement, demonstrates, however, that this axiom needs to be revised.

The axiom of local dependency has its base in legal and political theory of the immediate post–Civil War era, which saw the constitutional limitations on U.S. local government as highly restrictive. Justice John Dillon's 1872 treatise on municipal government formed the primary text for restrictive rulings throughout the nineteenth century (Gere 1982). Within the federal system, state governments delegated only limited powers to local government, and Dillon developed a distinction between the public corporation, which was relatively limited in its activities, and the private corporation, which was much less so. This truncated and dependent status, it has often been asserted, has continued to frustrate the proper and natural development of municipal government in the United States, leading some to account for a whole host of contemporary urban social problems as originating in the limited power of local government (Frug 1980). The story of nineteenth-century cities' fiscal behavior is thus familiar from textbooks: local abuse brought under control by firm application of the principles laid down in Dillon's 1872 treatise (Dillon 1872; Gere 1982; Frug 1980). In an echo of the U.S.

Constitution's delegation of nonenumerated powers to the states, policy derived from Dillon has consistently emphasized municipal government's dependence on state constitutions and legislation. Ideas about the fundamental power of U.S. local government have thus been shaped by this "strict" construction, reinforced by both state and federal court decisions down throughout the twentieth century.

The legal historian Lawrence M. Friedman has commented on the divergence in the law with respect to public and private corporations by the nineteenth century's end. Although by then the *ultra vires* doctrine — which held that a corporation could do no more than what it was specifically authorized to do — no longer applied to private corporations, "*ultra vires* never died for municipalities," Friedman notes (1973, 463).

In contrast to the legal paradigm, a second view — the rational, functionalist perspective on local government — stipulates that it is limited by design to respond to local needs, and that basic responsibilities of government not well handled by the state or federal governments can be delegated down to locales. The limitation on the power of local government thus conforms rationally to particular local circumstances: for example, a village, whose council form of government covers a wide but simple range of activities, may require only a single law-enforcement officer, whereas a large metropolis "needs" a broad spectrum of experts and a complex electoral system. State government, overseeing a range of local governments, accordingly delegates varied but limited authorities to each municipal corporation.

The rational-choice perspective on governmental limitation sees such layered responsibility and authority as corresponding to the nature of the economic decisions inhering in each level of government. Paul Peterson makes a persuasive case for this perspective (1981). Problems of free-ridership, for instance, can be overcome by allocating activities that give rise to free-rider problems to a level of government broad enough to obviate them. Public roads, for example, generate literal free-rider problems for the local government jurisdictions through which they pass unless the construction and maintenance of such roads is raised to a high level of aggregation, corresponding to the geographical and political boundaries of the users and other beneficiaries. Nineteenth-century farmers resisted building hard-surfaced roads because they considered the roads of greater utility to those on either side of their counties than to themselves (Barron 1989). Only by removing responsibility for and power to build certain kinds of roads from townships and counties could state governments overcome the free-rider problem.

Proponents of the rational-choice perspective might thus conceptualize the nineteenth-century constitutional limitation movement as a readjusting of local fiscal capacity to meet changing economic circumstances. Conversely, a federalist, legal perspective will view the process as an aspect of the state regulation of corporations, a process nested in the larger structure of a higher-level federal system. My argument takes elements of each, emphasizing that the restrictions' apparent squeeze on resources gave nineteenth-century local government powerful means for dealing with private sources of capital, helping build a limited, but nonetheless powerful, local state.

In the following chapters I combine quantitative analysis with examination of specific episodes in the history of city governments to illuminate the complex historical structure of the American local state. The primary concern is money. Thousands of local governments possessed the powerful corporate privilege of borrowing. Such loans simultaneously put property owners at risk and gave them hope of profit in the shape of increased land values. City borrowing offered investors the prospect of reliable local investments. By using their capacity to borrow to assist businesses, cities took out loans for, and purchased stock from, thousands of private enterprises. Voters, on the other hand, have always been stingy with their money and continually try to use it to get private enterprise to work for the public benefit.

The consequences of this local fiscal activity were multiple: most obviously, cities and towns got railroads, bridges, and factories. Although private enterprises, they accomplished public purposes. But they — that is, the voters and promoters in the cities and towns — also worried about their own proclivities to spend, and in the last three decades of the nineteenth century, they convinced state voters to regulate borrowing. As the new world of corporations unfolded, local governments both pushed in new directions and demanded external control. In so doing, they worked out the broad terms under which local governments functioned until the post–World War II era. This process occurred in local referenda on bond issues, in constitutional conventions, and in courtrooms.

The chapters that follow illustrate the long and intimate relationship between private investors and American cities, tracing the role of the courts and law in our urban fiscal history. And they explore some aspects of the rich and complex field of action and contention created by local finance for citizens, politicians, and private investors and entrepreneurs, in whose arguments, votes, secret deals, and, occasionally, desperate ploys the elements of the evolving American local state can be found embedded. The description and analysis of the local state forms a subtheme. From early on, indirect subsidies, avoidance of bureaucracy, and promotion of private enterprise characterized what might best be termed the "stateless state." These elusive attributes made it a state full of promise and hope, bluster and foolishness, at once flexible, adaptive, and even creative, yet also easily undermined by rhetoric and simpleminded herd behavior. For all of its flaws, it remains the local political and financial foundation upon which American cities and towns still operate.

CHAPTER TWO

Debt and Default

MEANING AND MEASUREMENT

> They were camped on the second bench of the narrow bottom
> of a crooked, sluggish stream. . . . Before them were a dozen
> log cabins, with stick and mud chimneys, irregularly disposed
> on either side of a not very well defined road. . . .
> "This, gentlemen," said Jeff, "is Columbus River, *alias* Goose
> Run. If it was widened, and deepened, and straightened, and
> made long enough, it would be one of the finest rivers in the
> western country."
> — Mark Twain and Charles D. Warner, *The Gilded Age*

A BUCCANEERING SENSE of political enterprise fueled U.S. cities in the century prior to the Great Depression. By borrowing large chunks of money, sometimes wildly, little towns and big cities alike tried to dazzle investors and residents with scenarios of wealth and opportunity. Mostly, the schemes worked. And when they did, bridges and factories appeared in towns. When the schemes failed, there were crises. The flamboyance and bombast of the Gilded Age may have owed more to the promoters of a strange public/private world than to the purely private sector, whose entrepreneurs have gained our attention ever since Matthew Josephson's *The Robber Barons* (1934). Lampooned in Twain and Warner's prescient novel *The Gilded Age*, promoters broke with what seemed to be honest practices and honorable traditions. They used local public corporations to promote schemes based on expectations of future expansion. These often airy schemes, nothing more than paper and imagination, violated what seemed to be common sense and public trust. And sometimes they resulted in fiscal collapse.

This chapter presents a historical perspective on the fiscal crises — in particular, those caused by the inability to meet debt payments — that have periodically visited American cities.[1] It endeavors to grasp the larger historical dimensions of American urban fiscal trends by following defaults on municipal indebtedness. This history is not the observation of annual balance sheets, which usually had to be in balance and directly reflected revenue capacity (Hardy 1977). The getting and spending of municipal money has from early on in the nineteenth century represented political choices that in turn declare a larger sense of city government's proper role. Because they were corporations, cities and towns could borrow, and the vehicle of debt enabled them to make vastly more dramatic moves than if their spending had been forced to hew to a strictly based revenue. Such debt provides a concrete index of a city's fiscal politics and is the outcome of a combination of social, political, and economic processes.

The research reported in this chapter both confirms and confounds conventional wisdom about current fiscal crises. The current state of crisis, which began in 1973 with the near default of New York City, is best seen as a return to the historical norm. Far from being something new, such crises have been occurring for over a century and were far more severe in the Depression of the 1930s. From this perspective, it is the period between 1945 and 1973—an era of unprecedented fiscal stability and expansion—that poses a problem for policy analysis, inasmuch as it deviated from a century-long tradition of fiscal uncertainty. Some thirty years of good times erased policymakers' memories of, and practical experience with, urban fiscal crisis—until the *New York Daily News* printed its famous headline "Ford to City: Drop Dead."

On the other hand, the research confirms the conventional wisdom that recent urban crises are different. Today's crisis is one of operating costs, not capital costs, and it is one over which the taxpaying populace exerts relatively little control. Earlier crises arose when cities borrowed large sums and deliberately chose not to spend their meager revenues on repayment. The Great Depression, for instance, was preceded by a dozen years of heavy capital borrowing and expenditures.

What emerges from the research presented in this chapter is a new sense of the fiscal aggressiveness that underwrote nineteenth-century urban expansion, and a reaffirmation of the depression's unprecedented disruption of local fiscal policy. In addition, we can see how the receivership model of handling crises eventually dominated a more creative and democratic, if unpredictable, crisis-resolution process. We might note that although then, as now, one side portrayed the debt holders as greedy vampires draining the city's lifeblood, while the other adopted a serious demeanor and spoke gravely of fiscal responsibility, belt-tightening, and cutting "nonessential" services, the nineteenth-century polemics on the subject sound more discordant than the arguments generated by New York City's 1970s crisis. Finally, this chapter shows that polarization around class, ethnicity, and financial and political interests has critically shaped struggles over municipal debt from the mid nineteenth century on.[2]

The fiscal landscape of nineteenth-century America buzzed with activity on the local level, and debt assumption financed much of the infrastructural expansion of cities and towns. The right to issue debt obligations was an essential feature of the incorporated city, and local infrastructural expansion was a significant means of underwriting the economic life of the locale. Yet for all the bond issues successfully retired, dozens of counties, cities, villages, irrigation districts, school districts, and other small governmental units defaulted or otherwise repudiated their debts. The assumption, repayment, or repudiation of local debt is thus a central, but wholly neglected, part of urban America's creation story.

This chapter both describes and analyzes the external dimensions of local fiscal instability in the United States from 1850 to 1936. It does so first by concentrating on two empirical goals: (1) to establish comparative magnitudes of urban fiscal stability from 1850 to 1936, and (2) to assess systematically the impact of the panics, recessions, and depressions of 1873, 1893, and the 1930s on fiscal stability, using the technique usually referred to as interrupted time-series analysis (see further below). Then, considered in this long historical context, the question of federal and local relations after the Depression and World War II is taken up. Considered in this way, the transforming impacts of the Depression, the New Deal, and World War II become starkly apparent. In effect, the federal-local fiscal balance established during the preceding century and a half was permanently altered in one fifteen-year period.

Defaults have been taken as a primary measure of fiscal crisis, partly because default is a significant and obvious identifier of crisis, and partly because the more complex municipal finance statistics available for recent years simply do not exist for the earlier period.

Because of nearly insurmountable data problems, the systematic statistical comparison of actual defaults over time cannot be carried past 1936. The Municipal Debt Adjustment Act of 1934, which was declared unconstitutional by 1936, enabled cities to use federal courts to declare bankruptcy and renegotiate their debt. It was the only New Deal legislation with the word "municipal" in its title according to Mark Gelfand, who finds it ironic that the act was never used by a city of over 30,000 (1975, 51). (Here it should be noted that in 1930, of the over 3,000 cities in the United States, only about 200 had populations larger than 30,000, so there were many more chances for smaller cities to use the new act.)

In the mid nineteenth century, as cities began to expand in population and number, they expanded their infrastructures and services. They also began a search for capital with which to finance these changes. Using their property tax streams as surety, they sold bonds, whose purchasers expected to earn interest payments and to have their principal returned at the end of some fixed period of time. Cities that could not or would not pay either principal or interest payments were considered to be in default on their bonds, and lenders had recourse to the law to get the money owed them. Lenders could sell their bonds, either at par or at a discounted price. If the bonds were in default, or the city's credit prospects were poor, knowledgeable investors could often purchase the bonds at bargain prices, speculating on the possibility that the city might pay the bond's par value at some future date. Not too surprisingly, cities often did not feel very great moral compulsion to pay off such speculators, particularly those who held bonds previously defaulted on that had been purchased from the often-desperate original owners at a price far below par. Some of the bonds issued by Memphis in the 1870s, for example, were resold for as little as 21 cents on the dollar, and the defaulting city later used this as a part of its justification for nonpayment. Somehow, the moral compulsion to repay diminished when payment would go to speculators and the actual lenders would never see full restitution.

In the late 1920s, Arthur M. Hillhouse (1935) collected the available data on all defaulted municipal bonds, which help form the basis for the statistical analysis in this chapter. No regular reporting of bond-payment defaults existed, and it was often in the interest of both the bondholder and the defaulter to hide a default, arranging terms in time for the city to be able to pay (see also Hillhouse 1936; Ridley and Nolting 1935; Betters 1933[?], 1936a, 1936b). Cities often used bonds for what we now euphemistically call "creative financing," and defaulting on the principal or interest payments of such "creatively" used debts often seemed scandalously willful. For example, the city of Watertown, Wisconsin, issued $200,000 of bonds to a railroad company that was to run tracks to Watertown from Madison. The record does not make clear whether the company resold the bonds or held them as collateral for other loans. The company failed, however, the bonds were sold at very heavy discounts, and when their purchasers sued Watertown for payment, the city refused to honor the judgment in favor of the bondholders.

To show the complexity of bond defaults, consider that a default can be either on a principal or on an interest payment. A defaulter on interest payments presumably could not pay on the principal either, but a defaulter on a principal payment might well have been able to make the smaller interest payments. A demanding creditor could help precipitate a default by refusing to extend the repayment period. Typically, a city unable to meet its principal payment sought new funding in order to make the smaller, more manageable interest payments. The amount of the default did not translate directly into an index of relative fiscal distress: a city unable to make a small interest payment might well be in direr straits than one unable to make a very large principal payment. Consider further the complication of measuring the amount of debt. Bonds were issued either for full-term maturity or for serial maturity. "Sinking funds," similar to escrow accounts, for the payment of bonds might be able to handle some, but not all, of the outstanding indebtedness, and such funds often themselves held the city's own bonds, purchased at heavily discounted rates.

The period analyzed statistically here, from 1850 to 1936, bounds the transition of the United States from a rural to an urban society. The proportion of the population in cities grew, in less than a century, from 15 percent to well over 50 percent. In this period, cities of all sizes and kinds discovered the use of indebtedness to finance their growing infrastructures. The issuance of debt changed from a rare expedient to the norm for cities. There should thus be at least three other annual series with which to compare an analysis of a series of bond defaults in this era: ideally, (1) urban population on an annual basis, (2) urban indebtedness on an annual basis, and (3) urban assets—that is, property values. Unfortunately, none of these annual data are available. Nor can they be created, unless one is willing to accept decadal interpolation for populations and guessing for the amount of debt.

These problems must be noted before the body of the analysis is begun, for they both illustrate the fragility of any data bearing on the topic and force a clear definition of the difference between historical analysis and financial analysis. The latter is undertaken to tell potential investors whether or not a particular bond issue is, or is likely to be, subject to risk. When companies rate a municipal bond offering today, the rating in part determines the costs of borrowing. It reflects the analysts' judgment of the municipality's ability to repay, a partially circular prediction, of course, because a poor rating will cause a municipality to pay more, and thus potentially be less able to repay. Financial analysis is almost the obverse of historical analysis, for past experience may be a very bad guide to bond risk. For instance, the city of Duluth and the Minnesota state legislature used legal maneuvers to cheat the city's bondholders of the early 1870s out of any hope of full debt recovery (see Chapter 5). The panic of 1873 wiped out the brand-new port's resources, and within five months, its population fell from 5,000 to 1,500 or even fewer. Some years later a recreated urban corporate entity began to issue new debt. Buyers of the new bond issue, although no doubt aware of the city's recent past, were naturally and exclusively interested in the city's future, and they bought the bonds. The city's history of nonpayment was almost completely irrelevant to them.

For the historian, on the other hand, the case of Duluth illustrates key aspects of municipal finance in the nineteenth century: the unpredictability of the short-term future, the willingness of state legislators to manipulate the law in favor of cities, the use of the law to create opportunities for capital investment, and the extravagant issuing of debt by cities to foster economic growth. Duluth possessed a port facility of modest but real utility, and although almost wiped out in the panic of 1873, the city rebounded quickly along with the larger economy. In contrast, private corporations existed only as fictional legal persons that could avail themselves of debt-issuing opportunities. Bankruptcy spelled out their character as legal fictions: for example, Jay Cooke and Company, which had precipitated the national crisis of 1873, simply ceased to exist.

Although the phrase used here is "municipal bond default," the defaulting political units varied in kind. Not all were cities or towns: 28 percent of the specifiable 941 pre-Depression defaults were by counties, 27 percent by cities, 21 percent by towns, 6 percent by local improvement districts, 5 percent by school districts, and 13 percent by miscellaneous unclassified units. Most such entities issue debt for what we would define as urban purposes, and for this reason it is important to include them in the analysis. In fact, by creative use of overlapping political entities, cities could often go well beyond any statutory limits on their legal debt obligations.

The most common kind of default was on bonds issued to support railroads. Some 35 percent of all pre-Depression defaulted bonds fall into this category. General obligation, improvement, and refunding bonds each accounted for 9 percent, streets and schools for 7 percent each, and irrigation, city buildings, waterworks, and aid to private enterprises other than railroads for another 4 percent. The remaining 8 percent fall into miscellaneous, unspecified categories. There are no systematic data on borrowing by local governments. We can neither estimate the number or value of the bonds at risk for each category nor determine the relative security or risk of these various funding purposes or issues. It is very probable, for instance, that well over 35 percent of all outstanding bond obligations were for railroads, in which case railroad defaults would reflect low rather than high risk.

Figure 2 plots the annual number of bond defaults by year from 1854 to 1936. Because the number in the Depression soared to such extremes, the inset graph plots the pre-1930 defaults on a scale that shows the variation of the earlier years more vividly. Prior to 1854 there had been only three bond defaults in the United States. Of the years between 1854 and 1936, only two went without a recorded default (1867 and 1869). In 1932, the *Bond Buyer* started reporting the number of defaults regularly. Most credit services and municipal information sources collected cross-sectional

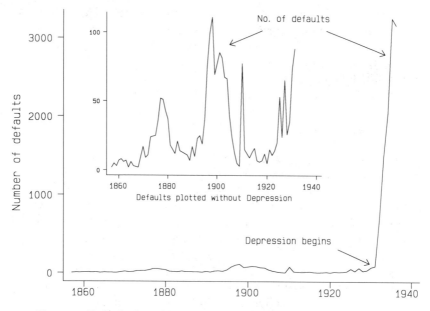

Figure 2. Defaulted municipal bonds, 1860–1940. Source: Monkkonen 1984a.

urban fiscal data, but they cautiously avoid naming the cities in default (Bird 1931, 1935). However these data do show the magnitude of the Depression, rising from 678 defaults in 1932 to a peak in 1935 of 3,251. The largest earlier peak had come in 1898, with 111 defaults.

This series plotting the proportional changes in the number of annual defaults displays apparent responses to depressions, each increasing in length of recovery time, interval, and amplitude. There also appears to be an upward drift in the series, but any adjustment for population at risk or amount of indebtedness would reverse the direction of this drift. Figure 3 represents one way of adjusting the raw number of defaults, converting them to a rate per number of urban places, the notion being that the more places there are to default should be the most consistent adjustment. Although a fluctuating series should be interpreted with caution, we can see an apparent upward movement until 1879, with fluctuation until the debacle of the Great Depression. In fact, a seat-of-the-pants analysis of the preceding 80 years suggests that the crises increased successively in magnitude.

The unadjusted counts of defaults per year in Figure 2 as well as the adjusted ones in Figure 3 suggest that depressions had large impacts on the pattern of defaults. In fact, the graphs appear to indicate that depressions — especially those of the 1870s and 1890s and the Great Depression — sent local governments into dizzying spirals of collapse. These visual impressions can be evaluated systematically using interrupted time-series analysis (McCleary and Hay 1980), which fits a univariate autoregressive model to a series of observations, then reestimates the model with the impacts specified. If the inclusion of the impacts improves the model, as measured by the diminished size of the residual — that is the unpredicted number (RMS, or Residual Mean Square) — then one can conclude that the

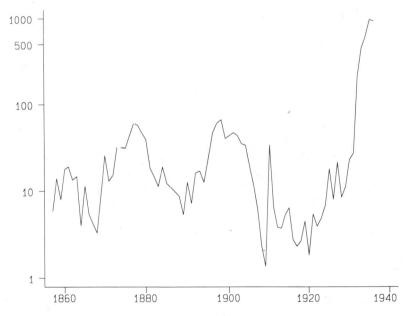

Figure 3. Defaults per thousand cities and towns, 1857–1936. (Note that these are plotted as logs to make them legible.) Source: Monkkonen 1984a.

specified impacts did indeed have a consequence. In essence, the time-series approach systematically detrends (or, makes "stationary") the series, predicting each year as based on all previous years.

Interrupted time-series analysis shows promise in the testing of hypotheses concerning the impact of specific events on a related time series. Given the kinds of statements historians often make about the impact of an event on some series of events, the technique seems to have obvious utility for historical research.[3] The only impediment to its application is that it usually requires at least 50 observations (that is, time units). An important aspect of time-series analysis concerns the nature of trend or "drift." Historians tend to conceptualize upward or downward movement in a series as a trend, the implication of which is that the underlying processes are changing in some regular and systematic way. The series is a "realization" of some less visible underlying process. However, as the end points and lengths of most series are arbitrary, a "trend" may actually be a deviation or random fluctuation in a larger unmeasured series. Not only historians are guilty of this confusion; for instance, the observed increase in crime rates of the 1960s and 1970s was widely interpreted as a trend by criminologists, yet historians using a longer perspective have seen this as a reversal of a centuries-old downward movement. Or, in the case of defaults, someone looking back in 1929 (the inset graph in Figure 2) would surely have concluded that city finances were moderately cyclical, with only a few more bad years coming before recovery. Instead of trend, time-series analysts thus use the concept of "drift," which requires a more open way of thinking about time-dependent events. It implies that any series may move up or down, but that without complete knowledge, the observer must perceive this motion as being similar to any drifting stochastic process.[4]

The question, once a proper univariate model of the series has been estimated, is whether or not adding in the information about the timing of depressions and recessions improves the earlier model's predictive ability. Even though the bond-default series has clear peaks in the depressions of 1873 and 1893, the added information about these two depressions makes no improvement in the model of the series. On the other hand, including the Great Depression does improve the model's fit. Thus, this impact analysis forces the rejection of the hypothesis that urban bond defaults simply marched in unison with larger crises in the economy. Although the analysis shows that while an economic catastrophe as severe as the Depression of the 1930s can have a resounding impact, the longer history of urban crises has been driven by forces other than boom and bust alone. Only the Great Depression caused a crisis of measurable scope, as characterized and measured by this time-series analysis of highly aggregated annual bond defaults. The other crises, although fluctuating in number per year, did not vary systematically enough to have any statistical significance. This overview of the worst moments in American cities' fiscal history thus shows a surprising degree of stability, or, more precisely, of insulation from external economic shocks.

Notwithstanding the surprising robustness of the local public/private political economy revealed by this overview, the Depression inaugurated sweeping changes. Local government expenditures grew rapidly during the 1920s, federal government revenues exceeded expenditures, and the Depression threw many taxpayers into arrears. Local government and the property tax levy formed the basis for much of the American state. In its specific manifestations, local government had grown even more varied in size and in legitimacy since the nineteenth century. Property tax was still the source of most governmental revenues, and in places where both the government's legitimacy and the equity of tax distribution were wildly distorted, tax strikes occurred.

In Chicago, political corruption took the form of "tax fixing" — illegal reduction of taxes for political purposes. David Beito shows that this occurred across the economic spectrum to an egregious degree. As delinquencies and conflict over tax payment came to be publicly disputed, the extraordinary variation in taxes was exposed, calling into question the city government's fundamental legitimacy, as well it should have. Tax inequalities as a result of political bosses granting property tax exceptions to favorites thus helped undermine the credibility of city hall. For nearly two years, the city met with strong legal opposition to its tax policies and suffered from high nonpayment of taxes.

The Association of Real Estate Taxpayers of Illinois (ARET), an organization formed in 1930, led the fight against excessive and uneven taxes in Chicago (Beito 1989, 44). Beito has analyzed ARET's membership to show that it was made up mainly of small proprietors, women, and skilled workers. Relatively widespread home ownership ensured that the property tax would be politically sensitive, while the Depression strained the average person's ability to pay taxes. But patently unfair tax distributions from neighbor to neighbor were nonetheless the precipitating element of the tax revolt in Chicago.

Tax revolts were more modest than might be expected given the extremely high unemployment during the Depression (around 28 percent). This can be attributed to several factors, including the quick public and legal responses to tax strikes, as in Chicago, where media campaigns and court actions ultimately defeated ARET. Payment of taxes also indicates that even when tested in a crisis, local government retained substantial legitimacy, achieved over a century of very carefully defined fiscal politics. Moreover, the political distance between the 1870s and 1930s was not as great as it seemed in the 1930s: Chicago's ultraconservatives saw tax strikes as radical, even communistic (Beito 1989, 65–66), and pro-business and anti-tax newspapers and leaders played roles in the 1930s crisis reminiscent of previous American tax protests, such as Shays's Rebellion.

The Great Depression shocked the public corporations of cities and towns as powerfully as it did the private corporations, but in very different ways. Private corporate enterprise, as a system, finally recovered. But local government as it had existed prior to the Depression never really recovered; instead, it was transformed. Of course, the century between 1830 and 1930 had seen local demands for state regulation of local government: but the state governments themselves never gained fiscal superiority or the revenue capacity of local governments. That is, when considered in aggregate, local governments had greater total revenues and expenditures than the states themselves. States principally entered the political economy as regulatory agencies, setting the rules, which local government then followed. When the Depression wiped out local credit, tax revenues plummeted, and as cities struggled simply to pay their previous obligations, borrowing became dangerous. For the first time, defaults skyrocketed beyond any predictability. The federal government, rich in resources, in large part because it did not do very much, was forced to take on a new role, becoming the cash-rich partner of local government. It also intervened by allowing city bankruptcy proceedings to occur under federal, rather than state, law, and in federal courts. This new mode has now survived 60 years.

Figure 14 in the Conclusion also shows one measure of this transition with startling clarity. From the Depression until the end of World War II, property tax revenues stayed at relatively similar levels. During the same period, the proportions of local budgets going to interest payments varied wildly as cities struggled to pay their creditors and then began to slip into default. Post–World War II prosperity ushered in a stable but very different relationship, indicated by rising property tax revenues and rising interest payments. The federal government made a dramatic new addition to the relationship, for it became a more powerful original funding source. Beito has discovered evidence that federal New Deal program administrators taught local government officers ways to avoid state tax and debt limits (Beito 1989, 142–43). An implication to be drawn is that federal administrators may have intended to alter local government's dependence on state regulation and to increase the local power of the federal government in a manner similar to Lyndon Johnson's poverty programs. In these actions, the federal government's agents consciously represented the reformers and modernizers, seeing local governments as provincial and benighted (see also Schulman 1991 for evidence of such feelings in the South).

Figure 4 displays the federal and property tax shares of local revenues. The graph requires careful consideration. First, note that both lines connect percentage contributions from two sources, and that they do not sum to 100 percent after the Depression as more local revenues came to cities from state governments or indirectly from the federal government. Second, note that the horizontal axis loosely corresponds to year, but that it actually plots the per capita amount of local revenues on a log scale. Local revenues have risen with a few exceptions since 1902, hence the correspondence with year. The graph shows local and federal contributions to city revenues approaching equity in about 1960. More than that, the graph makes clear the negligible role of federal money until the New Deal. Most significantly, the graph demonstrates that the shift to

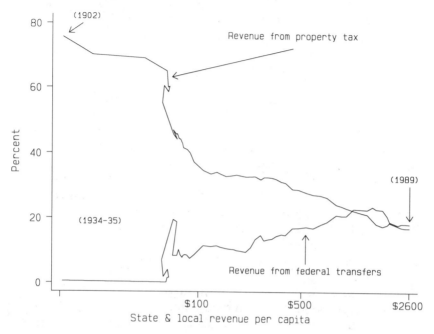

Figure 4. Estimated proportions of state and local revenues from property taxes and from the federal government, by per capita revenue, 1902–89. Sources: *1977 Census of Governments*, vol. 6: *Topical Studies*, no. 4: *Historical Statistics on Governmental Finances and Employment* (Washington, D.C.: USGPO, 1978), supplemented with annual data from *National Income and Product Accounts of the United States* (Washington, D.C.: U.S. Dept. of Commerce, Bureau of Economic Analysis, USGPO, annual).

heavy federal contributions has occurred in the context of dramatically increased local revenues. That is, with the exception of the 1930s, the lines continuously drift to the right, or to higher and higher revenues.

Yet before immediately drawing further conclusions about the altered local-federal fiscal arrangements, one must also consider how the changing proportion of the population living in cities affects the nature of local-federal relations. In 1930, at the beginning of the transformation, about 56 percent of the population lived in places with over 2,500 inhabitants, a figure that may have decreased slightly during the early Depression, and that did not dramatically alter until after World War II. The urban transformation of the United States resumed at the end of the war, when the proportion of the population living in cities and under local governments resumed its century-long climb. The federal government itself slowly came to represent an urban nation. Thus the federal role in revenue allocation among local governments has come to be distributive among cities, rather than distributive from rural to urban areas or vice versa. Accordingly, the change in local revenue mix reflects in part the changing urbanization of the United States, intermingled with the necessarily altered role of the federal government as tax collector and spender.

The federal government's local role becomes an open question, for although it is a visible and much larger presence after 1930, its action at the local level is highly ambiguous. States still retain their constitutional power over cities. The federal role inheres in its rules on taxation and expenditure. The best-known example here is President Lyndon Johnson's War on Poverty and the much-discussed "maximum feasible participation" rule, designed to frustrate unfair local politics. One could say that this exemplifies the federal strategy of providing a carrot rather than using a stick. From their onset, New Deal programs were often locally administered, used various cost-sharing formulas, and in appearance simply aided or steered local efforts. The interpretation of these programs and their thousands of follow-ons has been one of increased central power.

Yet one might interpret them very differently: local governments gained power and independence as their revenues become less dependent on local voters. When local taxes were the primary source of local revenues, local politicians had to be very cautious. Accordingly, when local taxes became only one of several components, local politicians may be seen as gaining in autonomy. Local governments thus declined only in appearance, and in fact actually enhanced their power and independence of the electorate. In this view, then, one otherwise puzzling aspect of Figure 4 disappears, for local revenues on a per capita basis have grown enormously in the postwar era, especially when considering that the plotted values represent only a portion of all local revenues. The power of local officials has increased both financially and in independence from local fiscal control.

Urban fiscal conflict and action has taken place in widely various and subtle contexts. The issuance and repayment of municipal debt is far more than merely a mechanical outcome of routine accounting, borrowing, and funding, and this is particularly true of the nineteenth century. Fiscal crisis—a city's inability to make a scheduled debt payment—must in the final analysis be considered a Janus-faced indicator. Default looks outward and inward, reflecting both the national economic climate and local conflict, the growth and decay of capital, political accord and conflict. Provided one remains aware of the national context, a city's "bottom line" can give access to internal dramas of power, resistance, and innovation. Our image of urban finance in the nineteenth and early twentieth centuries may be drawn from quaint, sepia-toned photos of clerks with gartered shirtsleeves and eyeshades, but the accounts over which they presided may yet be made to reveal the central passions of the city.

CHAPTER THREE

The State Politics of Debt Restriction

THE CASE OF ILLINOIS

> The extreme ease and facility with which towns, counties and cities are voting away hundreds of thousands of dollars to irresponsible paper railroad companies, and even to private manufacturing establishments, is fast becoming a matter of grave concern and alarm amongst thinking men.
>
> — *Ottawa Republican* 10, March 1870
> (Illinois Historical Survey, "Cole Notes")

ILLINOIS, "The Land of Lincoln," with its rich agricultural and industrial assets, its broad political spectrum, and its wealth, is a state that encompasses a broad realm of American experience, providing the ideal case study for those interested in industrial, urban, and agricultural development. In its smaller cities, Illinois encompasses the complex tangle of local initiatives that has typified American industrial growth, and it provided a model for other states in dealing with local government.

State Constitution Remaking: A Background

The details of this model first took shape at the Illinois constitutional convention in 1869. The existing constitution was 30 years old: very old by the standards of American states. Much legislation in the nineteenth century consisted of specific, personal bills, and state constitutions were remade relatively frequently in response to changing economic and demographic circumstances. There had been an attempt at writing a new Illinois constitution in the midst of the Civil War, but its anti-Lincoln, copperhead Democrat proponents failed to get it ratified. The state split on the issue of civil rights for freedmen, something unacceptable to the southern counties, which were very southern indeed.

When they gathered in Springfield in the early winter of 1869–70, the 84 delegates to Illinois's constitutional convention could look forward to a long five months of intense debate and discussion. For the politics of the time, they were a diverse group: 47

Republicans, 33 Democrats, and 4 independents.[1] Their average age was 45. The two youngest members were just 23, and William Patterson of Kankakee died during the convention at 40, but one-fourth were over 63. All were prominent men in their communities. Eleven called themselves farmers. Most of the others were lawyers and merchants, but they were hardly big-city folk, for many came from very little towns. O. H. Wright, a 41-year-old lawyer, was from Havanna, population 1,785, the seat of Mason County. Westel Sedgwick, a 42-year-old lawyer, was from Sandwich, population 1,844, in DeKalb County. And James Poage, a merchant, came from Aledo, population 1,076, in Mercer County. They and the newspaper reports about the convention claimed that their diversity and varied backgrounds lent the document they drafted its weightiness and credibility.

In the 1840s, following the panic of 1837, a rage to revise state constitutions had swept across the United States. The new constitutions deliberately curtailed state governments' abilities to build their economic infrastructures, severely limiting future state investments in enterprises such as the Erie Canal (Gunn 1988). The classic American pattern—state promotion of private enterprise for the public good—suffered the first of many attenuating political mood swings.

Like New Yorkers, who first took the initiative in limiting state debt in the 1840s, Illinoisans limited their state debt in the antebellum era. The state's constitution of 1847–48 mandated a phasing out of *all* state borrowing. The state's debt peaked at $16.7 million in 1853; by 1870 it had dwindled to $4.9 million, and by 1881 it had disappeared. The state was debt-free for the next forty years (Illinois 1926, 645–46).[2] But these seemingly Draconian constitutional actions did not end government involvement in the economy. Rather, they shifted it to the county and municipal level.[3] This shift in the location of public debt, which remained essential for large, risky capital enterprises, came just as the roles of the corporation—both public and private—and the city expanded (Hartog 1979; Teaford 1975; Monkkonen 1988). Consequently, the locus of power for government-backed economic activity expanded, diffused, and became more flexible. At the same time the local governments to which it dispersed were themselves gaining new powers.

One intention in shifting debt issuance to the municipalities from the states had been to ensure more attentive and informed voter control of governments' fiscal activities. This had one clear implication — fiscal conservatism. Ray Gunn (1988) has shown, for instance, that the main impetus behind New York State's more restrictive constitution was the popular desire to limit state power. Thus the actual expansion of local fiscal power through newfound abilities to issue local debt occurred as the unintended consequence of a broad political desire to constrain the public sector. Gunn plots this consequence as an irony. In the pre–Civil War era, the economic shift toward a more capital-intensive industrial and managerial mode prompted voters and citizens to put the state apparatus under constant, if contradictory, pressure to underwrite and promote the new economy, while at the same time remaining limited and locally accountable (Schieber 1982; Galambos 1983; Pisani 1987). The built environment reflected this change, as thousands of new county courthouses and city halls became more important than state capitol buildings (Lebovich 1984; Johnson 1977; Peet and Keller 1984; *Courthouse Conservation Handbook* [1976]).

Since voters and governments ought logically to have provided all encouragement to economic growth, one is tempted to assume that the latent power of state governments to promote development and change was not fully exploited *by choice*. But this simultaneous promoting and restricting has often characterized the American state and does not negate the underlying modernization process. If it did, then by implication one might claim that the antiregulatory, and often fiscally straitened, American states of the 1990s are unmodern.

The Civil War showed the flexibility and power latent in local government even as federal power grew dramatically. While Washington levied an income tax, municipalities in the North raised troops by issuing bonded debt to pay enlistment bonuses (often the equivalent of several years' pay). Postwar voters and politicians quickly damped these demonstrable powers, however, ending the federal income tax and turning their attention to the issue of local debt in a manner reminiscent of the 1840s.

The Illinois Constitution of 1870

In ratifying their new constitution of 1870, Illinois voters turned from the antebellum issue of state debt to the postbellum issue of local debt. Why did political leaders and voters agree to limit both the kind and the amount of debt local governments could incur? Did they really want to get rid of the goose that laid the golden eggs? By any measure the state and its economy had prospered under the prior arrangements.

Delegates to the constitutional convention focused on municipalities' common practice of using bonded local debt to raise capital to attract and capitalize railroads. By 1869, every person in the state was responsible for $4.05 of bonded or subscribed debt — the largest chunk to railroads. This debt was not evenly distributed though, for 36 of the 102 counties, including Cook County, had no railroad debt.[4] To particularize and reinforce their restriction on the amount and purpose of local debt, voters overwhelmingly ratified a separate article, submitted with the constitution, forbidding local government support of private railroad corporations. On the face of it, the major link of the public/private system had been shattered.

Illinois was one of the earliest northern states to establish such limits, although nearly half of the other states followed suit in the following decade. Michigan and Ohio had restrictions that required positive legislative approval; Iowa's 1857 constitution limited local debt and forbade extending credit to railroads (it also forbade banking), but an 1868 statute expressly authorized local taxation to aid railroads (see Gelfand 1979, 549; Iowa 1857; Iowa 1868). This confusing development allowed taxpayers to make direct subsidies, but did not allow the incurring of future obligations. In effect, it also reduced the initial amount of any subsidy, although presumably a railroad could capitalize this promised cash flow. Illinois imposed its debt limits in the context of a national movement to control Civil War debts, local corruption, and very heavy local public investment in railroads.

In other states, most notably Massachusetts, legislatures began to mandate some limitations of local indebtedness in the 1870s. Massachusetts, arguably the most modern of the American states, never constitutionally limited debt as did Illinois and the majority of other states. In 1869, Illinois towns were only slightly more indebted, to the tune of $15.74 per town dweller as compared to Massachusetts's $14.95 (Illinois estimated with weighted means). (Clifford Blunk [1926, 118] asserts that Illinois's mean debt was $14.68 in 1870, citing Illinois 1926, 645, as his source; however this source reports *state* debt.) By 1870, Illinois local debt seems to have risen substantially to $22.00 (although this difference had no measurable impact on voting patterns).

More typically though, states attempted to control local debt through constitutional amendments, either by setting specific limits, like Illinois, or by directing state legislatures to set limits. Even today little is known about the effectiveness of debt limitation, some experts claiming that it is ineffective, others that it is. "It is generally believed that debt restrictions have not significantly restrained the total volume of state-local borrowing. To avoid these limits, special districts have often been created . . . [resulting in] an increase in the cost of borrowing" (Aronson and Schwartz 1975, 234). In a detailed study of Massachusetts, Royal van de Woestyne (1935) concludes that ceilings were "effective," but he also speculates that they gave some cities' debt issuance an upward goal, thereby increasing local debt. More to the point, he points out that Massachusetts granted over 1,500 exceptions to its own legislated debt and taxation limits between 1875 and 1911. But whether or not it has been effective, debt limitation has been a popular way for states to respond to what they see as uncontrolled local excesses.

Earlier, in 1862, one article of a new constitution proposed by an Illinois constitutional convention had stipulated that no county, city, or town could lend its credit or subscribe to any private chartered company or corporation, including railroads. Voters rejected this constitution for reasons having nothing to do with debt (black suffrage was the issue), and subsequently, in 1869, the legislature funded all preexisting local railroad debt by returning state-collected tax monies to local governments so that they might pay off their locally contracted debt. The constitution the voters ratified in

1870 included a railroad-debt restriction similar to that in the rejected 1862 constitution, and an overwhelming 134,114 to 34,067 approved the section forbidding local funding of railroads, which was submitted to the vote separately, but voted on at the same time.

In addition, and of more long-term importance, the new constitution itself limited all municipal debt to no more than 5 percent of assessed property value. Some Illinois cities had had debt limits written into their charters. Chicago's, for example, was $100,000 in 1850 (Einhorn 1988, 184). Yet separate allowances compromised this seemingly absolute limit — a school tax (an additional 0.20 percent property tax), a general revenue allowance (another 0.35 percent property tax), a debt-repayment tax (a further 0.05 percent property tax), yet another 2 percent tax to build a lake barrier and city hall, and an additional allowance for borrowing to build a marketplace. If this were not complex enough, three years later, the legislature granted the city authority to borrow $100,000 for a waterworks and to raise its property tax for debt repayment to 0.1 percent (Appendix A, Chicago).

Quincy's even more fluid cap set the interest on debt at no more than "one half of the city revenue arising from taxes, assessed on real property," which in turn were capped at 0.5 percent of the assessed value of real *and* personal property (Illinois 1840, article V, sections 1 and 3, 116–17). At 5 percent interest, this would translate into a 5 percent debt limit, at 4 percent into a 6.25 percent limit, assuming that the bonds sold at par. By 1841, new legislation allowed Quincy an additional 0.125 percent in taxes for schools, doubled to 0.25 percent for schools and 0.28 percent for gas lighting in 1859, both perhaps also raising, even doubling, the already blurred initial debt limit. And other cities had even more open debt provisions: legislation enabled Galesburg, for instance, to raise "requisite" sums to build county buildings, the only limitations stipulating interest of no more than an astonishingly high 10 percent on twenty-year bonds (Illinois 1863, sections 1 and 3, 173).

More generally, Illinois towns and cities utilized the charter and legislative process to select from a repertoire of limiting devices. Of course, most places chose not to limit themselves at all, at least formally. None forbade any specific kind of enterprise — such as a railroad or a factory — requiring local debt. Of the 301 towns and cities in Illinois, 129 had statutory debt or tax restrictions similar to the Chicago, Quincy, and Galesburg examples. These limitation histories can be surveyed through Illinois statutes prior to 1870. They have an ad hoc, scattered quality that suggests an easy flexibility, coupled with attention to minutiae. The devices cities chose reveal their concerns, which clustered around four themes.

First, many choosing not to limit debt did limit the interest payable and demand that bonds be issued at par, clearly an attempt to avoid exploitation, profiteering, and, perhaps, corruption. Sixtythree of the 301 cities and towns had explicit debt provisions in some form, although it is very difficult to discern if these were targets rather than ceilings.

Second, those setting debt ceilings did so at dollar amounts rather than at some proportion of property value.

Third, tax ceilings varied considerably, from as low as 0.5 percent to at least as high as 1.5 percent (Chicago by 1863). When at the lower limit, this was only for general taxes, with other designated taxes, such as taxes to fund schools, allowed. Of the 301 cities and towns, at least 124 had some sort of property tax limit.

Fourth, in addition to revenues from taxes, licenses, fines, and fees, towns usually required all males over 21 to work for three days on the streets or pay for a substitute, at a rate sometimes specified at $1 per day. Statutes required that the donated labor be of high quality. This regressive tax could be construed the equivalent of a 1 percent income tax. Of the 301 cities and towns, at least 95 had a street-labor requirement.

These statutory limitations are summarized in more detail in Appendix A. Because they have had to be discovered by reading sequences of Illinois statutes, they represent an undercount. Many of the differences may be trivial, and they certainly are, as Lawrence M. Friedman has observed, "irritating and confusing" (Friedman 1973, 460). But they do make clear that cities and towns did have fiscal limitations prior to the constitution of 1870, and that these varied. Taxes were raised and lowered; debt limits were set and then abolished.

This varied menu of rules for local finance produced equally varied fiscal outcomes. One way to see this is to consider a county's taxable wealth (as measured by its assessed property values) contrasted to the actual borrowing practices that it and its villages and cities had been following. By using data gathered in preparation for the constitutional convention in tandem with other data collected by the state auditor, the ratio of these values can be summarized. For the whole state in 1869, the mean debt/assessed property value ratio for all counties, adjusted for population, was 2 percent, while ten counties had debt/assessed property value ratios of over 5 percent; the highest, that of Cook County, stood at 16.5 percent.[5] Had custom or law stipulated a standard practice or even a range of standard practices, this ratio should be tightly clustered around some central value, but instead, like so many other features of local finance, it shows considerable sweep. Legislative debt limitation had proved as flexible as the Quincy example suggests. As with railroad debt and the vote, excepting Cook County, there is virtually no statistical relationship between debt/assessed property value ratios and the vote.

These actions present a puzzle: How could voters have flown in the face of what seems to have been their self-interest in promoting their own local economies? Why did they put a ceiling on their own ability to support private enterprise, ending direct local subsidization of railroads? Some commentators have suggested that the haves (Chicagoans, for instance) essentially voted out the have-nots (more remote counties that still'had few or no railroads or capital development) (Newell 1904, 495). But only 7 of the state's 102 counties voted for liberal debt-issuance policies. The overwhelming majority wanted to restrict local debt capacity. The demand for restrictions bespeaks the context: a conflicted public view of fundamental law's role in simultaneous promotion and control; unexpected partisan positions on this conflicted view; the quick transit from concept to action in using the law to manipulate the local political economy; and the origins of American voters' ambivalent relationship to their own financial power and obligations.

The National Pattern of Local Debt Limits

The default cases discussed in Chapter 2 have already made clear that local political considerations pushed political factions to manipulate city debt obligations. In addition, much of the evidence presented in that chapter establishes good grounds for believing that local political circumstances, as well as internal and external economic constraints, determined defaults on municipal debt across the United States over a long period of time. The time-series analysis also demonstrates that only the Great Depression of the 1930s had a clearly identifiable impact on this variation.

Because not every state limited debt, it is possible to begin to understand the consequences of the debt-limitation movement even before clarifying its more detailed explanations. A view from the national perspective suggests that the presence or absence of limits made no difference whatsoever in local debt levels (see Appendix B for the exploratory regression analysis of national data for 1870 and 1880: it shows that debt limits had no effect on the level of state debt). The strong implication is that debt limits and debt itself were not really linked; public money and attitudes toward it were two different phenomena. This finding needs further refinement, using data in cross section for every governmental unit, rather than simply for the states. This can be done using published census data for 1880, in which local debt is enumerated in a format paralleling the 1869 Illinois survey used later in this chapter (U.S. Census Office 1884).

These figures indicate that across the nation, local debt grew absolutely but declined in per capita terms from 1870 through 1880 and into 1890. In 1870, counties had contracted debts totaling $187.5 million. Cities and towns exceeded this considerably, for a total of $328.2 million. The per capita county debt burden was about $4.86, and the local debt burden about $39.60. By 1880, the county per capita debt had fallen to $2.50, and it fell again to $2.30 by 1890. It is unclear if this decline was actual or an artifact of different reporting methods, for the total county debt rose substantially between these decades. Local debt rose to $701.9 million in 1880, and to $761.2 million in 1890: just as for the counties, this represented a slight per capita decline (these values are calculated from U.S. Census Office 1872b, 11; U.S. Census Office 1892, 57).

The comparative per capita figures are approximately $23.80 for 1880 and $21.90 for 1890: it is difficult to state this figure in precise per capita terms, for there is no way to know the exact base populations of cities responding. The two values reported above for 1870 and 1880 are more reasonably accurate, for the Census Bureau reported the population bases of all cities that also reported their debts. There is no doubt that the comparative figures for 1880 and 1890 are deflated, but they have been deflated by the same unknown amount, so are thus comparable to each other. The 1880 census contains a table summarizing indebtedness for places over 7,500 people and gives per capita figures by state, with the population base representing only that of reporting cities. Reported in this way, the average net debt per capita is $51.09, but averaging obscures a considerable range between states, from $2.62 in Colorado to $127.66 for Washington, D.C. (U.S. Census Office 1884). In summary, while our knowledge about the national context of local debt in the late nineteenth century is limited, there is the strong implication that per capita local debt declined.

As Illinois prepared for its 1870 constitutional convention, the state auditor collected information from every county on the kind and amount of its municipal debt. Even though there was no national correspondence between debt and debt limits, one might nevertheless expect to find such connections within individual states. On the face of it, one would expect to find a series of strong relationships between kinds and amounts of local debt; the presence of vigorous cities and towns in a county; the strength of the local tax base — urban and agricultural; and the votes on the constitution and the section ending debt for railroads. Surprisingly, this is not the case: randomness is suggested by virtually every scatterplot and a correlation analysis.

For instance Figure 5, displaying total debt — city, township, and county — by total county population, shows that with the exception of the top six or seven cases, there is a widely dispersed scatter between county population size and all local debt. As the amount of debt grew (horizontal axis), county population (vertical axis) neither rose nor fell. The two box-and-whiskers plots along the sides of Figures 5–8 show the median, quartile, and 95 percent points of each single distribution. Illinois townships could elect to remain dissolved in county government or be independent political units, electing officials and collecting taxes (Carr 1987, 196). (See Appendix C for the correlation matrix.) This suggests that the population of a county alone had no simple visible relationship to the amount of its indebtedness.

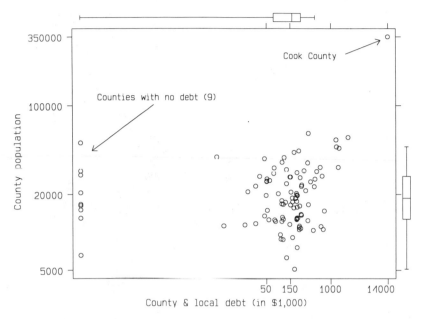

Figure 5. Illinois county population and total debt (log scale), 1870. Sources: Illinois 1870c, 100–105; U.S. Census Office 1872a, 23.

Nor does the debt of a county appear to have any relationship to that of the cities and towns within its borders, as demonstrated in Figure 6. As city and town debt in each county grew (moved to the right on the horizontal axis), the county's debt neither grew nor fell. Again, if we were to ignore the six counties with the greatest local debt, there is little evidence that an increase in county debt is likely to be associated with a corresponding increase in local debt. Certainly, these data do not allow us to assert that there was a unitary political culture or practice of borrowing, for debt-free towns could lie in high-debt counties and vice versa.

When we turn to taxes, the lack of a strong relationship between segments of the fiscal units is similar (R^2 excluding Cook equals 0.34; more sensibly, on a per capita basis, it equals 0.11). These plots also make clear that at nearly one-third of a million people, Chicago's size makes it a potential distorting factor in statistical analysis, and in all of the analyses that follow, care has been taken to

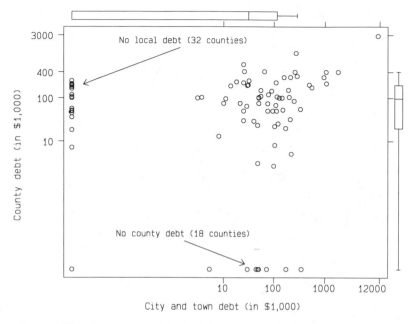

Figure 6. Illinois county and local debt (log scale), 1869. Sources: Illinois 1870c, 100–105; U.S. Census Office 1872a, 108–21.

compensate for such distortions. Figure 7 shows it in relation to the other 101 counties of Illinois with respect to the 1870 property tax and total debt. The log scaling in the graph keeps Cook County near the others. The image locates this exceptionally large economic concentration in a congruent relationship to the other counties, in the sense that it is not down in the lower right-hand corner of the picture. The image shows that the nine debt-free counties paid a range of property taxes not all that different from those counties with substantial debt. (Mean taxes for the non-borrowers were $107,850 — $4.98 per capita — and for borrowers, $131,330 — $5.80 per capita.) Revenue capacity did not determine who borrowed and who did not. Economic status alone did not, therefore, determine borrowing.

Figure 8 enlarges a portion of Figure 7 with Cook County excluded (and the upper left quadrant of Figure 5 blown up, county names rather than symbols plotted): it shows much more evenly distributed values with three counties, Sangamon (containing Springfield, the state capital), McLean, and Peoria counties (printed on top of each other) giving the illusion of a positive correlation between taxes and debt. In all statistics reported below, the regressions were run dropping each outlier county sequentially, using a statistical test (Cook's D) to measure the county's possible distorting influence.[6] At this point it is worth reiterating the lesson to be drawn from Figures 5–8: no obvious relationship between local indebtedness and taxes obtained in Illinois. Even what should have been the strongest and least problematic association, that between population size and amount borrowed, was rather loose.

Nine Illinois counties — Boone, Calhoun, Clinton, DuPage, Jersey, Marion, Morgan, St. Clair, and Stephenson — had no debt whatsoever in 1869. Of these, Calhoun had no towns and a population

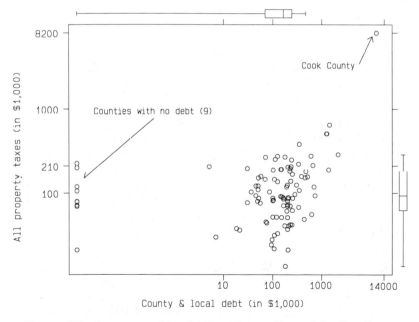

Figure 7. Illinois county and local debt and taxes (log scale), 1870. Sources: Illinois 1870c, 100–105; U.S. Census Office 1872a, 108–21.

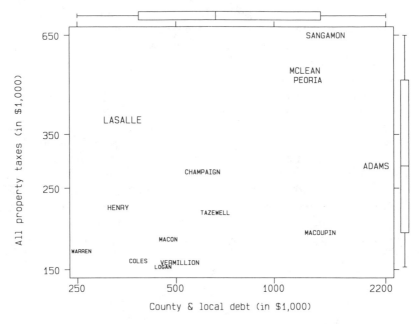

Figure 8. Illinois counties with high debt and taxes, 1870. (Cook Co. dropped; log scale; county name plotted and scaled to population.) Sources: Illinois 1870c, 100–105; U.S. Census Office 1872a, 108–21.

of only 6,562, while St. Clair had nine towns and a county population over 50,000. Such measures do not give a sense of underlying fluidity: one year later, only two of these nine, Calhoun and Marion, still reported no debt. On the other hand, Bond, Crawford, Edwards, Moultrie, and Putnam counties, which had previously reported debt, now reported none at all.

There were, then, two extremes among the counties of Illinois. On the one hand, there was enormous Cook County, with well over a third of a million people, who had collectively borrowed nearly $15 million; on the other, there were parsimonious, debt-free jurisdictions like Calhoun and Marion counties (with no villages in Calhoun, and just two small towns in Marion). Illinois contained just over 300 municipalities, ranging in size and political power from Chicago to tiny hamlets of a few hundred people, and what made the potential local corporate power so threatening was the fact that small places could act independently. That the average population of these 300 places was only 500 persons was not as important as the fact that nearly a third (30 percent) of the state's population lived in them, and not on farms, and by virtue of living there had access to municipal power without limit.

In the Convention

Any theory attending to economic development, the law, and the state would highlight the role of personal as well as economic characteristics in seeking to understand why people took the positions they did on development issues. In this case there was a well-understood purpose to the uses of local debt, for the law's power lay in creating opportunity and in controlling debtor-creditor relationships through the courts. In theory, younger, Republican, Yankee, and non-farmer delegates should have opposed constitutional limits on local debt-issuing power, which was a key tool in promoting local economic expansion. These were, after all, the pro-development, commerce- and industry-oriented people — "modernizers" or "go-getters." Surprisingly, in almost every way this turns out not to have been the case.

Party identification was crucial in the discussions of the delegates elected to the state constitutional convention and their votes on local railroad-debt questions. One might expect that the Republicans, the pro-business and modernizing party, would have been more likely to support local initiatives for lending (McCormick 1986, 173, 296). After all, the subsidization of railroads and other local businesses benefited many business people and railroad lawyers directly. But in fact, the ostensibly fiscally conservative and antimodern Illinois Democrats were more likely than the Republicans to support unlimited local debt, perhaps befitting their relative poverty or the economically backward locales from which they came.

In Table 1, I estimate logit equations predicting the delegates' votes for and against the section of the proposed constitution seeking to restrict local debt to 5 percent of assessed property value (12 against, 38 in favor, and 34 abstentions). The estimate shows that

TABLE 1
Delegate Support for 5 Percent Limit on Municipal Debt
(N = 84)

Variable	Coefficient	Std. error	t	Prob > |t|	Mean
For					.45
Democrat	−2.36	.57	−4.12	0.00	.39
Farmer	−.33	.72	−0.46	0.65	.13
Constant	.66	.32	2.08	0.04	1
Against					.14
Democrat	3.24	1.13	2.87	0.01	.39
Farmer	2.84	1.17	2.43	0.02	.13
Constant	−4.35	1.11	−3.93	0.00	1

SOURCES: For votes, Illinois 1870c, 599; for delegate information, Illinois 1870b, 176–78, supplemented with county histories on file at the Illinois Historical Library.
NOTE: In the "For" category, Chi-square (n = 3) = 21.60, probability = 0.0000, log likelihood = −47.04; in the "Against" category, Chi-square (n = 3) = 19.27, probability = 0.0001, log likelihood = −24.81. The following scoring system was used: Farmer delegate = 1; New York or northern birthplace = 1; Democratic affiliation = 1. In the "For" category, a vote in favor of limitation = 1; an abstention or a vote against limitation = 0. In the "Against" category, a vote against limitation = 1; an abstention or a vote in favor of limitation = 0.

Democratic affiliation (40 percent of the delegates) more than tripled the likelihood of a delegate opposing the limit (see the coefficient for Democrats in the lower panel of Table 1).[7] Contrary to what one might have predicted for the more "modernizing" Yankees and younger delegates, neither age nor place of birth bore any relationship to the vote in the convention. Farmers did have a somewhat different opinion on this policy in contrast to the great majority of delegates (lawyers, bankers, and merchants); they were nearly as likely as the Democrats to be *against* the limit. Either the farmers were not fiscally conservative or debt limitation was not the fiscal conservative's choice.

In the convention debates, only two farmers, both of whom ultimately voted no, entered the discussion on the article. Both boarded at the Revere boarding house, where 6 of the 11 farmers (as opposed to only 8 of 74 non-farmers) stayed (Illinois 1870b, 176–78). William B. Anderson of Jefferson County spoke only to seek clarification of a word (Illinois 1870a, 1241), and the other farmer, James G. Bayne, a Republican from Woodford County, explained his opposition to a substitution requiring a two-thirds vote as a part of the article on limitation: "I do not consider it as republican, since it requires a two-thirds vote, when, as I suppose, the true principle is that majorities rule," he said. He went on to propose that "only actual residents will vote. There will be a fair expression of the real residents, and if they choose to levy a tax for a railroad, or school, or canal, or other purpose, and the majority vote for it, I have no doubt that it will be a proposition that will advance the interest of the county, town, or school district interested" (Illinois 1870a, 1239).

Joseph Medill, a Republican newspaper editor, who was leader of the Chicago delegation, offered the most detailed and principled articulation of a stance on this issue, speaking vehemently against Bayne. "I am surprised," he said, "to hear some of my friends on the left affirm the doctrine that voting subscriptions or gratuities to railways, or in aid of local improvements, is a matter that interests nobody but the particular locality that so votes." He then developed a position that fully reflected John Dillon's recently enunciated doctrine that municipal governments were not sovereign and could only act in fiscal matters subject to the "direct and express Power of the State" (Illinois 1870a, 1239).

Assessing support for debt restriction as rural or antipromotional is thus highly inaccurate: Democrats, who in principle favored a limited state role, also wanted their local governments to adopt a hands-off attitude.[8] And here the complexity of the issue emerges. Anti-state and anti-entrepreneurial ideology could be translated into permissiveness in fiscal control, not so much for permissiveness's sake as to avoid state government interfering with local voters. And, conversely, the modernizing, pro-business group could be cautious in trying to implement its vision of state economic promotion.

Ratification of the 1870 Constitution

The new constitution encountered great voter apathy, perhaps reflecting its ostentatiously nonpartisan construction, for voter turnout in Illinois ordinarily resulted from militantly organized partisan efforts, voters literally marching to the polls (Shortridge 1981). (See Argersinger 1985–86 for a discussion of voting fraud:

that the vote on the constitution was bipartisan may have decreased fraud and turnout. This disinterest parallels that exhibited in New York in 1840 [Gunn 1988].) One study estimates the number of eligible voters in the state in 1870 at 625,139; half that number turned out for local elections in 1870 (Hansen 1980, 204). In stark contrast, fewer than one-fourth of all eligible voters turned out to decide the state's new constitution.[9]

Because the vote for the constitution was recorded county by county, rather than at a more local level, one cannot discern precisely how various local polities voted. But there is a substantial amount of information at the county level, so that variations in local borrowing practices, local taxes, and property values may be estimated. In this section, I use these measures to recapture the surrounding fiscal circumstances that might have affected how voters dealt with these financial issues. To untangle these murky signals, I have estimated a regression model, reported in Table 2.[10] The model is intended to capture the impact of relevant local circumstances on the voters' ratification of the section to limit debt. Prior to discussing the model, a separate consideration of the voting picture helps set the scene.

Figure 9 displays each county's vote for limiting lending to railroads by the amount of taxes it paid. Rather than use the actual number of votes, I have followed the convention of converting the number to log odds, which can be interpreted as the chances of voting for or against the constitution, the zero point reflecting an evenly split vote.[11] A county's wealth usually determined its taxes. In Figure 9, the horizontal line represents the point at which votes split, fifty-fifty, on the article on railroad debt. The plot suggests only a loose association between a county's wealth and its voters' support for lending limitation. (Actual correlation is a modest R^2 of 0.09.) In Figure 9, the county's name, scaled to its population, is plotted, rather than another symbol. The typical counties, that is, those with similar voting and taxation, blur into an overprinted cloud of names, while only the very different counties stand out from the crowd. Large and wealthy Cook County is highly visible, while Boone County, a small, agricultural northern county whose residents paid low taxes and strongly supported debt limitation, appears in tiny print in the upper left quadrant of the picture.

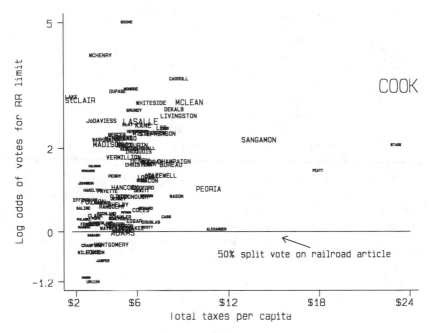

Figure 9. County support of railroad lending limit by taxes, 1870. (County name plotted and scaled to population.) Sources: Illinois 1870c, 100–105; Illinois 1870a, 1894–95; U.S. Census Office 1872a, 108–21.

Populous and aggressive Adams County (with the city of Quincy), on Illinois's western border, paid high taxes and was very divided on the question of debt limitation. And only a handful of counties actually had more voters against the lending article than for it: Figure 9 makes it clear that they were relatively small and paid low taxes.

The dependent variable in the model is voting for the special section of the constitution forbidding issuance of debt to railroads. While in all counties this differed only trivially (a few voters did not bother to vote on this section) from the vote on the constitution itself, it seems to me that it captures more purely the sense of local debt limitation.

Figure 10 displays the economic and political measures that best capture the voting context. The upper left pictures the vote per capita property taxes: this is the same information as in Figure 9, with outliers — Boone, Hardin, and Macoupin — deleted. Other relationships appear to be equally modest. The variables used to predict the votes are all uncorrelated with each other. Diagnostic tests confirm that none of the pictured straggling counties had unduly distorting effects on the statistics.

Five different variables best capture the local context. The tax per capita variable indicates both the wealth and the tax load of a county. On a per capita basis, it suggests just how widely varied the different counties were, ranging in tax load from a low of $1.73 a person to a high of $23.34 (in Cook County), with a mean of $8.40. This variation is a combination of land value (farm and city) and of the voters' willingness to pay taxes on that land.[12] Other variables of importance include whether or not the county sent a Democrat to the constitutional convention, the subscribed debt (that is, money

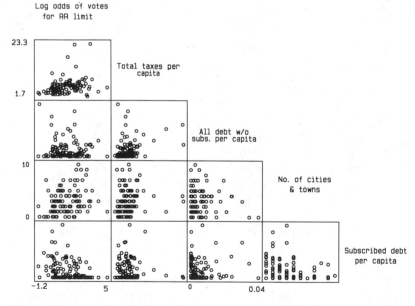

Figure 10. Matrix plot of regression variables: votes, taxes, debt, and towns, 1870. Sources: Illinois 1870c, 100–105; U.S. Census Office 1872a, 108–21.

TABLE 2
Estimate of Economic and Political Support for Debt Limit
(sum of weight is 2.4884e + 006)

Source	SS	df	MS	$N = 99$
				$F(5, 93) = 25.24$
Model	88.64	5	17.73	Prob $>$ F = .0000
Residual	65.32	93	.70	R-square = .5757
				Adj R-square = .55
TOTAL	153.97	98	1.57	Root MSE = .84

Variable	Coefficient	Std. error	t	Prob $> |t|$	Mean
Log oddvt					1.76
Tax pc	89.98	16.37	5.50	.000	.0084
Democrat	−.82	.20	−4.17	.000	.37
Sub. debt	−35.63	12.61	−2.82	.006	.0049
N towns	.10	.04	2.68	.009	3.56
Debt pc	−30.66	18.30	−1.68	.097	.0047
Constant	1.26	.27	4.62	.000	1

SOURCES: For votes, Illinois 1870a, 1894–95; for delegate information, Illinois 1870b, 176–78; for political affiliation, financial data, and votes, Illinois 1870c, 3–5, 100–105, 599; for population data, U.S. Census Office 1872a, 108–21. See Appendix C for further details.

ABBREVIATIONS. SS, sum of squares; df, degrees of freedom; MS, mean square; MSE, mean square error; log oddvt, log odds for vote; sub. debt, per capita subscribed debt; debt pc, per capita debt; tax pc, per capita tax; N towns, number of towns and cities in a country; tax pc, per capita tax; sub. debt, per capita subscribed debt; debt pc, per capita debt.

NOTE: Three counties—Boone, Hardin, and Macoupin—were identified as outliers using Cook's D and were excluded from the regression.

not yet actually borrowed), the number of municipalities in the county, and, but only very slightly, the actual amount of local debt. The equation in Table 2 demonstrates the good fit of the model; over half of the vote is "explained" by these five variables.

The table's coefficients may be interpreted as showing that two variables positively predicted the votes for debt limitation: property tax per capita and number of towns in the county. In other words, the wealthier the county, and the more it thus paid in property taxes, the more likely its voters were to place limits on the local fiscal capacity. In addition, the more political units capable of borrowing — that is, the number of cities and towns — the more likely voters were to support debt limitation. Areas most able and likely to borrow most favored the curtailment of borrowing.

On the other hand, the greater the local subscribed debt, the more likely voters were to turn *against* the limit. And if the voters had sent a Democrat to the convention, this tendency was further amplified. Late-nineteenth-century Democrats are a puzzling lot; we still have much to learn about them, as opposed to the political cultures of antebellum Democrats or their populist contemporaries, for whom there exists ample historical research. Their attitudes seem so firmly entrenched in the past as to make them a half-century behind the times—deliberate "old fogeys," like the residents of Oquawka, Illinois, about whom we learn in the next chapter.

These results suggest that in spite of the overwhelming sentiment in favor of limitation, voters in counties that used debt for promotional purposes did not want to end their option of supporting further railroad development. Actual debt seems to have had a slightly opposite effect to subscribed debt, but the low t value in the table forestalls any strong interpretation of this effect. I interpret the seeming contradiction in the effect of taxes and debt as indicating that the support for increased debt came from those locales where government really did use it, but only when taxes and, by implication, assessed property values, remained low.

In a consistent pattern, voters and their delegates showed that the concept of debt limitation had little to do with the state government's control of local finance. Nor was it an attempt to detach government from local corporate enterprise. Instead, the issue had to do with the amount of local support for business. And the new constitution enacted limits relatively consistent with the older, but much more flexible and ad hoc, statutory ones drawn up for many towns. There was one very big exception: railroads. The new constitution put an abrupt stop to the vigorous local financing of railroads, and in so doing, it must significantly have affected the further extension of local tracks. Does this reflect a local perception of overbuilding, or, more likely, the perception that municipalities were engaged in a market that they could not control, and in which they were forced to bid mercilessly against one another? If so, no evidence survives.

CHAPTER FOUR

The Local Politics of Debt

LIFE IN THE STATE OF PARTIES AND COURTS

> Oquawka hesitated, and this was her evil hour. Her light was
> hid under the half-bushel of old fogeyism, railroads were
> driven from her doors and decay set in.
>
> — Quincy *Herald,* January 7, 1871

 THE RATIFICATION of the Illinois constitution needs to be set in three additional contexts. The first is that of the counties, where the voters lived, where their experience of local debt was debated and felt, and where constitutional rulings on debt had their impact. The second is that of the consequences: most simply, the new constitution provided a legal basis for action in the courts. And approximately every other month, for the next two decades, a case involving local borrowing reached the Illinois or federal Supreme Court. The third is the locus in which the federal Supreme Court and the town — including local entrepreneurs, lenders and borrowers — contested the larger political and constitutional issues.

The Local Context: Case Studies

What did not happen is as important an element of the local government's fiscal politics as what did happen. The voting analysis in Chapter 3 has shown how, all else being equal, locales that did not borrow more strongly supported constitutional debt control. The least fiscally active were more vigorous in imposing their standards than the most, yet permission to borrow does not necessarily mean counties actually did so. Because the historian's attention is attracted by flashy "natural" events, the big court cases, the big borrowers, and the noisier actors, there is real potential for neglect of the less contentious, the non-borrowers, and the quiet. Sometimes they should be excluded, of course, but here such bias would exclude elements essential to the making of the modern fiscal state.

Figure 11. Illinois study counties. From top to bottom: De-Kalb, Fulton, Adams, Cumberland, Marion, Gallatin, and Massac.

Out of a possible 102 Illinois counties, I have examined the local political/fiscal histories of 7 (plus a supplementary one) with a view to compensating for such omissions and bias, and to provide local contexts for this analysis. All the counties were selected without prior consideration of their visibility in federal Supreme Court records or the other historical annals, such as they are, of fiscal history. To ensure that they were as broadly representative as possible, I chose them on the basis of multiple criteria, including location (they are dispersed throughout the state), debt, the predictability of that debt, and the county's proximity to the other study counties, mean state debt, mean population, and mean number of towns. One study county, Gallatin, turns out to have had a town, Shawneetown, embroiled in an attention-grabbing court battle over its debt similar to those used as illustrations throughout this book. I make no claims as to the scientific adequacy of this sample, except that it does represent a broad range, and that it definitely was not opportunistically chosen. As a consequence of this sampling strategy, only very fragmented and thin primary sources of details of some counties' local political economies could be unearthed. The fiscal narratives of the seven sample counties—Adams, Cumberland, DeKalb, Fulton, Gallatin, Massac, and Marion—highlighted in Figure 11, range from the most complex, Adams, to the very brief, Marion. I deal with the intricate Adams County first, as the issues it embodies in turn become relevant in all of the others. (See Appendix D for a fuller discussion of the county selection criteria.)

ADAMS COUNTY

On the west central Illinois border, the Mississippi River flows between wealthy Adams County and the state of Missouri. Quincy, the county's bustling, economically diversified urban center, lies about fifteen miles upriver from Mark Twain's home town, Hannibal. The county's two representatives at the 1870 constitutional convention—Orville H. Browning, a former Whig turned Republican, and Onias C. Skinner, a Democrat—both supported the constitutional limits on municipal debt, unlike the county's voters, who split almost evenly on the question. (This placed them with the small group of more divided counties.) Typecasting these two as either anti-railroad or opposed to economic development, based on their votes, would be erroneous. Skinner, for instance, was a classic local entrepreneur and railroad booster. His one term as a state supreme court justice had earned him the lifetime title of Judge, at least in Quincy. At 52 he had been "elected by democracy of Adams County a delegate to the Convention to remodel the constitution of Illinois" (Redmond 1869, 295). According to a contemporary, Judge Skinner was "full of public spirit and enterprise, he was among the earliest advocates of our railroad system, and having aided in the completion of the three roads that at present enter the city, he is now President of a fourth, the Chinook and Carthage Railroad, which by his energy and tact he has placed upon the road to speedy construction" (Redmond 1869, 295).

Although the other delegate, Orville Browning, did not appear to share Skinner's politics, he too represented the local elite. He was "one of Quincy's most illustrious citizens," a leading railroad lawyer, politician, and a principled antislavery Republican (Collins and Perry 1905, 386). A friend of Lincoln's and an ex-Kentuckian, Browning had moved to the state in the 1830s and risen with it to prominence and wealth. He had had personal experience with Judge John Dillon, the American authority on cities and the U.S. Constitution, appearing in federal circuit court before him to defend the Chicago, Burlington, and Quincy Railroad against Iowa's rate-fixing legislation (Baxter 1957, 263). A convinced racist, Browning turned anti-Republican on the issue of black suffrage. He began to consort with Adams County Democrats after Lincoln's death, and when they were persuaded of his antisuffrage stance, accepted their nomination along with Skinner (Baxter 1957, 214).

Quincy was an aggressively entrepreneurial and somewhat fractious place of 24,000 people. The city had successfully pursued the classic American route to economic achievement by borrowing large sums to subsidize its key businesses, especially railroads, and taking the considerable risk in bad times of paying its debts in scrip, which it in turn funded with more bonded debt. Although Browning and Skinner supported the restriction of debt at the convention, they made sure that the restrictions applied only to debt contracted after the constitution was approved, insisting that Quincy's most recent railroad aid bonds be specifically exempted. Browning chaired the convention's municipal corporations committee, which drew up the debt-limit section and article. He makes no comment on this committee's work in his diary (Randall 1933, 266). Browning and Skinner's city borrowed aggressively until the very last opportunity. Consequently, Quincy had a large debt, and no contemporary local commentator could fail to address the issue.

As the constitutional delegates worked in Springfield, the Quincy *Herald* thoughtfully discussed the city's debt, its prosperity, and its successful competition with other cities. The *Herald* (a Democratic newspaper) took pains to remind its readers that "we have a debt that may not be looked upon in the light of a blessing, but we must admit that from the same many blessings have come to us. . . . It is what has made Quincy and given her position and wealth" (January 7, 1871). To make its point, the editorial contrasted Quincy with Oquawka, about fifty miles ("one thousand," joshed the editorialist) upriver. "Twenty-five years ago it was perhaps the most prosperous city on the Mississippi. . . . [But with the coming of railroads,] Oquawka hesitated, and this was her evil hour. Her light was hid under the half-bushel of old-fogeyism, railroads were driven from her doors and decay set in." The editorialist contrasted Quincy with other nearby Mississippi river towns — Keokuk, Hannibal, and Warsaw. By lending money to railroads and building an economic infrastructure, Quincy's "mercantile interests prospered under a new order of things. . . . Manufactories sprang up and the din and bustle of business upon our streets was soon equalled by the hum of industry and activity in the mills, factories and workshops that were fanned into existence by the prosperous winds that followed the inauguration of our railroad system." Apparently the question of debt and local economic promotion did not deter the newspaper from attacking any national taxes and the tariff associated with Republicans, which it assailed as "legalized robbery" (May 25, 1871). This separation of local debt for economic promotion versus national debt for redistribution (the Civil War debt) sounds surprisingly similar to Paul Peterson's analysis of local and nonlocal governments in *City Limits*. In so clearly articulating the logic of local promotion, debt, and economic growth, the editorialist shows that Quincy's leaders explicitly understood how business and law — read, government entrepreneurialism — worked. It was the modern way of doing things: the alternative was the "old fogeyism" and stagnation of Oquawka.

Economic promotion did not translate automatically into other forms of political modernism. Only a year earlier, the *Herald* had urged its readers to vote against the constitution, primarily because it did not explicitly deny suffrage to blacks (June 26, 1870). At the time of ratification of the Illinois constitution, the paper's virulent racism almost drowned out all other issues, but it did manage to mention that the constitution wrongly prohibited lending money to railroads and wrongly proposed to limit the amount of all local debt. But for this Democratic party mouthpiece, debt was clearly a minor issue. Partisan resistance to the Republicans, centered for the most part on the issue of race in its national context, dominated the pages of this paper until ratification. "Modern" capital promotion and the promotional use of the local state coexisted quite happily with racism in Quincy.

Quincyites must have worried that their forward-looking attitudes might lead them into uncharted and dangerous waters. Many of their knowing pronouncements show signs of repressed uncertainty, an uneasy bluster about local debt and economic growth. Henry Asbury, an old-time Whig, best reveals this underlying anxiety in his *Reminiscences*. In 1881, when there was serious political talk of debt repudiation in Quincy, with the city actually refusing to pay some of its more questionable obligations, Asbury reminisces on the subject in agitation rather than tranquility. In about 1880, Mayor John K. Webster, a prominent banker and realtor, had refused to pay both unregistered debt and money owed to the water and gas company. The courts backed the latter default, as the debt had been contracted after the ratification of the 1870 constitution and was therefore illegal. The company dismantled both fire hydrants and stopped gas production, leaving the city without light for over a year (Collins and Perry 1905, 192–93; 551–52).

After defending Quincy's debt as the engine of its economic growth, Asbury slides into citations of Magna Carta (Asbury 1882, 201), Illinois Supreme Court decisions on local debt, and a series of metaphors and stories, each of which further obscures the debt question. He next rambles into a hopelessly inane, but also deeply revealing, racist story in dialect: "Now with all due respect to our Supreme Court and its decisions upon these municipal bond questions, we are reminded of a story told us by a venerable colored gentleman all of the oldest kind we knew in Kentucky." From this Asbury deviates to "the 'city goose' which lays its golden egg each day in the lap of honest labor," which "shall not be killed by unwise and exorbitant taxes at the hands and for the support of mere political loafers." He concludes this metaphorical and logical muddle by remarking on the "forbidden fruit [which] for us was city debt" (Asbury 1882, 205–6).

Although Asbury's allusions and precise intent may be impossible to untangle, he does identify the major constellations of meaning for the local political economy: fundamental law and the Illinois Supreme Court's interpretation of it, party identification, economic growth, city services, taxes and debt, and voters. Through this bundle of issues runs an undertone of apartheid. At least for men like Asbury, racial attitudes paralleled debt attitudes. Against slavery, but also against black suffrage, they favored local state development through borrowing, but opposed unrestricted borrowing privileges.

Like Asbury, the voters of Adams County and Quincy identified the issues involved in local growth. Such forward-looking entailed ambiguities and risks, however, and racism put them at odds with the national constitutional transformation of the Fourteenth and Fifteenth Amendments. One wonders if it was their partial embracing of modernization that left Quincyites so threatened by their own desires and beliefs even as they pulled ahead in the race for prosperity against losers like the residents of Oquawka (whose population is still under 2,000).

FULTON COUNTY

Fulton County, although about forty miles nearer Chicago than Adams, lacked Adams's urban, industrial, and transportation advantages. Notwithstanding its large population, Fulton's farms were relatively poor. Its delegates to the convention — Lewis W. Ross, 57, and Samuel P. Cummings, 50, both Democrats — voted against limiting local debt, but the voters in the county had other ideas, voting two to one in favor of limiting debt. The *Fulton County Ledger*, a Democratic newspaper published in Canton, followed delegates Ross and Cummings in trying to push its readers toward an active political economy. It tried to inspire them by telling the story of how their namesake town, Canton, Ohio, "trebled in population, quadrupled in wealth" following its loan to a mowing-machine manufacturer. A "good hotel building" and the machine shops of the Toledo, Peoria and Warsaw Railroad would be the right start for Canton, Illinois; otherwise, the paper feared, the town would "soon be so badly dried up as to need fencing in to mark the spot on which she once stood" (January 31, 1868, 2). On the fifth page of the same issue, the paper congratulated a south Fulton County township for voting (314 to 21) to subscribe $30,000 to the Chicago, Burlington and Quincy Railroad (which, unfortunately, picked another route in the next few months). In a year the town got a bill passed that authorized its stock subscription in the proposed new hotel (*Ledger,* February 5, 1869, 2). Today Canton has nearly 15,000 residents.

By the early summer of 1870, with its time running out as the new constitution neared ratification, Canton had begun to take more action to aid a railroad. In a final effort to whip up interest, the *Ledger* reminded its readers: "The road will be built. If Canton don't give handsomely, the road will pass a few miles north of the town, and thus do us a great injury, by drawing from us a large amount of trade" (June 3, 1870, 2). The town called for the referendum just three days before it voted on the constitution. In the same column in which the newspaper urged its readers to approve the $100,000 railroad subscription, it called on them to vote against the new constitution, and in particular against the article limiting municipal loans to railroads. In part the *Ledger's* position was partisan; it argued on July 21, 1870, that the draft constitution was Republican and favored black suffrage. The same issue reported defeat of the railroad subscription, 369 to 263, and blamed farmers for the negative outcome.

The voters subsequently ignored the recommendations of the *Ledger,* voting for the constitution and its railroad limits; only the nearby hamlet of Farmington voted no. Canton finally did put up some money for the Pekin and Mississippi Railroad, $6,000, in 1872, through subscriptions from citizens; these same enthusiasts worked to raise additional monies through higher property taxes (*Ledger,* March 29, 1872). But they had missed forever the opportunity to use the town's corporate borrowing privileges to entice railroads.

MARION COUNTY

The Illinois Central Railroad cut through Marion County, in south central Illinois, the only county in this study located there. A second major railroad, the Mississippi, cut through Marion from Vincennes, Indiana, in the east, to St. Louis in the west. The county's principal newspaper, the *Centralia Democrat,* took a predictably partisan stance in favor of low taxes and no tariff.[1] Centralia, a purely railroad town founded by the Illinois Central in 1853, grew with its shops, and with additional economic input from local coal mining and processing of farm products. The town tried to use its debt-issuing privileges to attract the Southern Illinois Normal University with a grant of $75,000; failing that, it bid the same amount for the Chester and Centralia Railroads (*Centralia Democrat*, May 27, 1869, and April 23, 1870). Only 52 percent of the county's voters wanted to limit lending to railroads, but this must perhaps be interpreted as an ignorant stance on development rather than a moderate one.

MASSAC COUNTY

Massac, a county at the very southern tip of Illinois, the region known as "Egypt," split its vote in the same proportion as Marion. Its newspaper, the *Metropolis Times* (Democratic), made the case for lending to railroads explicit and clear (April 16, 1868). The county had no railroad, the Illinois Central running about thirty miles to the west. Farmers in Massac lost 25 percent of the value of their crops for lack of a railroad, some said. A proposed donation of $200,000 in county bonds "will not increase our taxes. Within three years of the completion of the Road now projected, our taxes will be less than we are paying this year. Our numbers and wealth [will] be increased and our county expenses cannot be any more than at present, and divided between so many, we won't feel it half as much as we do now," the *Times* argued. Within a year, the county had upped its offer to $300,000, claiming that it was virtually on an "air line" (i.e., as the crow flew) from Chicago to Memphis and the Gulf of Mexico (*Times*, June 3, 1869). The newspaper neglected to mention the very large matter of the Ohio River — on the banks of which the county's main town, Metropolis, was sited. There was no bridge, and the county never managed to make good on the promised loan.

To supplement Massac County's fragmentary record, I include here material on an adjacent rural county, Gallatin, just to the north. In an effort less extravagant than Massac County's and equally unsuccessful, Gallatin County's Shawneetown — an old riverbank village subject to frequent floods, about forty miles up the Ohio from Metropolis, and with fewer than 2,000 inhabitants — also tried to generate capital to attract a railroad. "Shawneetown promises to become what it should have been years ago — a great and

powerful commercial and manufacturing point," its boosters proclaimed (*Directory, Charter and Ordinances of the City of Shawneetown*
[1872], 7). The town had, in fact, earlier subscribed to $25,000 in
the stock of the St. Louis and Southeastern Railway, the contract for
which required completion from Shawneetown to the Illinois Central by October 1870. The construction did not go quickly, and the
city council extended the contract deadline to 1871. The railroad
had established regular service by 1872. To contain the periodic
flooding, the town invested another $50,000 in a levee.

In spite of these efforts, Shawneetown did not prosper (it never
got a bridge over the Ohio, and its population remains under 2,000
today), and its debt thus became burdensome to the taxpayers.
Eighteen years later it finally defaulted on the debt payments, the
debt holders sued, and the Illinois Supreme Court declared the
bonds for the debt invalid. The court took this position based on
the timing of the debt extension granted after the passage of the
1870 constitution, which, after all, had invalidated all new loans to
railroads (*Eddy v. People*). The magic formula of growth was not
infallible; locational disadvantages could invalidate the rhetorical
ploy that declared any place between one big city and another to be
on the main route.[2] Shawneetown followed the seemingly successful road to growth, only to be defeated by nature and a location that
no booster's rhetoric could easily overcome.

DEKALB COUNTY

DeKalb County, just to the north of LaSalle County and the small
city of Ottawa, lay fifty miles straight west of Chicago (for more on
Ottawa, see Conzen 1987). A prosperous Republican county, with
small villages and a strong agricultural sector, it voted heavily in
favor of the constitution and its debt limits (the vote ran 95 percent). Nevertheless, the county's main newspaper contended that
by providing a direct north/south connection between Superior,
Wisconsin, on Lake Superior, and New Orleans, the Belvidere and
Illinois River Railroad would enable farmers to avoid the "extor-
tions of Chicago warehousemen," and that tax revenues from the
railroad and its appreciated property would more than cover the
initial cost of supporting it (*Sycamore True Republican*, April 27,
1870). A glance at a map shows this argument only to be true if

proved with a bent ruler: moreover, the assertion ignores the obvious proximity of somewhat more attractive railroad termini (i.e., those in Chicago). Of more interest than the tortured geography is the stance of this otherwise Republican newspaper, which by partisan logic should not have urged local voters to support more railroad debt. Evidently the *True Republican*'s editors were able to discriminate between the Republican party platform and the prospect of economic growth.

Case Law

It was the potential for court action that gave the new constitutional limits their bite. And, like the independent political dynamics of different Illinois counties, the many cases in which cities were actually taken to court for violating the new constitution show that partisanship and local economic circumstances lay behind voters' actions. What happened when profligate spending was held up to the close scrutiny of courts? In order to examine how the courts interpreted the constitutional restrictions on debt, I have analyzed the 146 Illinois and U.S. Supreme Court cases dealing with contested municipal debt (see Appendix E). All originated in Illinois in the second half of the nineteenth century.

Most Illinois cases involving municipal debt in the nineteenth century came to the higher courts in a decade and a half falling between 1870 and roughly 1890: these fifteen years encompassed about two-thirds of all cases.[3] Figure 12 plots the number of cases per year, showing the burst of post-constitution activity, first at the state level and then, about a decade later, at the federal level. The new article in the constitution may not have caused this burst, but it certainly played a role in the new cases.

Of course, not all disputes about local debt had to do with constitutional limitations; they were also about a myriad other problems. However, a surprising number of the disputes did involve debt limitations, either explicitly or implicitly. Typically, modern commentators have concluded with finality that the U.S. Supreme Court favored bondholders, while elected state judges favored repudiation (Warren 1935, 678; McGrath 1963, 210; and especially the discussion in Fairman 1971, 918–1116).[4] They argue that state

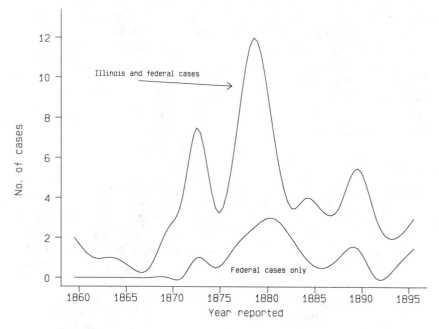

Figure 12. Illinois court cases on local finance, 1859–96. (Spline function plotted.) Source: West's *American Digest* (1902), sections 3, 13, 14, and 15 (see Appendix E).

judges acted more in the interests of local political and economic elites, while federal justices had risen above such parochial pressures and concerns. But the pattern for Illinois modifies this scenario: few state cases actually went to the U.S. Supreme Court, and seemingly antimunicipal decisions were actually the outcomes desired by the locales. In many of these 146 cases, the new state constitution played a significant role: on at least 37 occasions, the court explicitly cited limitations imposed by the 1870 constitution.

These cases make it clear that the apparently restrictive constitutional limit actually gave cities and towns a powerful tool to use against their creditors. Debt limits functioned as legal tools enabling municipal corporations to deal with failed projects. In two-thirds of the cases (about 95), the trial outcome had the practical consequence for the municipality of determining whether or not it repaid its creditors. In varied ways, about 55 cases involved munici-palities refusing to repay debts for which there had been inade-quate performance by the funded enterprise. In these 55 cases, the judgment invalidated the original debt, with the consequence that the municipality did not have to repay the loan. Cities consistently argued a debt's illegality — that it had been contracted above and beyond what was permitted by the constitution — to escape their contractual obligations or avoid payment to nonperforming private enterprises.

Virtually no cases came at the urging of uninterested enforcers concerned about the politics or ideology of debt limitation. More to the point, no municipality that had promptly paid an illegal debt ever appears on the court dockets. Nor did illegal debt ever come to court where the purpose of the indebtedness had been accom-plished. In other words, the supreme courts saw no cities that had contracted debts over their limits but that repaid the debt holders in a timely manner.

Cases that terminated in the Illinois Supreme Court usually con-cluded with a municipality not having to pay its creditors (44 versus 15), whereas those that went on to the U.S. Supreme Court had the opposite outcome (19 versus 4). But because most cases stopped at the Illinois Supreme Court (105 versus 32), the general outcome of all cases where debt repayment was at issue was that municipalities did not have to pay. It is important to remember here that not having to pay came as the result of a municipality's debt being declared illegal, an outcome that, if casually read for its surface meaning, would seem to be against the town's interests, and that would seem to invoke the constitution to curtail local fiscal capac-ity. This interpretation, however, misconstrues both the constitu-tion and the courts as antiurban.

Very much like the burghers of Hamelin in Robert Browning's popular "The Pied Piper of Hamelin" (1880), taxpayers in the late nineteenth century tried to avoid paying their debts if they thought they could get away with it. The poem tells the story of a medieval town government that promises to pay a piper for ridding the town of the rats consuming the grain that is the stock-in-trade of its mer-chants. He does, but once the problem is gone, the town council refuses to pay what it has promised, and the piper retaliates by piping away almost all of its children. Most Illinois towns were not quite as greedy and untrustworthy. To their credit, the majority did not really try to cheat; they simply refused to pay those who had not delivered as contracted. Perhaps Browning captures contemporary doubts about such promises, and most city councils could not see themselves as siding with the mayor of Hamelin's declaration: "Besides, our losses have made us thrifty; / A thousand guilders! Come, take fifty!" But those who wanted to avoid payment had a way perhaps unavailable in Hamelin, and certainly unavailable prior to legal limits on borrowing: they could claim that they had had no right to borrow the money in the first place.

This seems to be what Bishop did. This tiny agricultural township in south central Effingham County (fewer than 600 people, and under 150 voters) voted (44 to 22) to borrow $10,000 to aid the Springfield, Effingham and Southeastern Railway on the same day that it turned down the 1870 constitution, 42 to 20.[5] At least 7 voters were fickle, for the vote on the special article on railroad aid was 35 against and 27 in favor.[6] Testimony intimates that there was fraud involved in the petition for the special election, at least as regards 2 of the 25 names supposed to be on it. The petition itself, hastily put together by a railroad entrepreneur the night before the deadline, was posted in only two places, at one of which it had been hurriedly pinned to a fence post with a peg whittled on the spot.

The whole of Effingham County voted overwhelmingly in favor of limitation. Thirteen years later, the railroad did get built, but it ran into financial difficulties. Declaring bankruptcy, it demanded its $10,000 from Bishop. The citizens no longer wished to repay the money, perhaps because they knew that the railroad had no piper, perhaps because they hadn't read Browning, or perhaps because the original election had been less than democratic. Lower-court materials include several lists of names: the original 25 petitioners, the poll-book list of 70 voters on the constitution (alas, not with their votes), another poll-book list with 62 voters on the $10,000 donation (yet 66 tallied votes!), and the list of 143 claimants on the bankrupt railroad. Poll books allow an estimate of the lower bounds of electoral inconsistency, for we may compare who showed up to vote on the varied issues, if not how they voted.

The poll books do not quite sum properly; there are too few

voters in the bond vote, too many in the vote on the constitution. Even more peculiar, only eleven petitioners for the railroad voted at the special election. At least two people, Perry Nelson and Samuel H. Smith, signed the petition for the bond election, came to vote on the constitution, but did not vote at the same time on the actual bond issue. Another, William Field, voted on the railroad bond but not on the constitution. Given that at least seven others voted for the bond issue but against the principle of aid to railroads, one gets the sense of an election somewhat less aboveboard than might at first appear. Perhaps there was fraud, or perhaps it was an issue handled sloppily because only a handful of people cared. The list of 143 claimants in the bankruptcy proceeding against the railroad shows no overlap with the voters on the original issues, so at least we can conclude that there was no direct profiteering.

The case came on appeal to the state supreme court in *People v. Town of Bishop* (1884). The court first had to decide when the new constitution had taken effect. After a lengthy discussion—which takes two pages to summarize in the case report—the court concluded that the constitution had become effective on sundown on election day, simultaneously with Bishop's vote to lend the money. Therefore the donation was not prior to the constitution and not valid. Consequently, Bishop did not have to repay the money. And perhaps it is just as well the county never became an industrial center. Slightly over a century later, local economic development has recently put Effingham (but not Bishop) back in the news. The county seat is now selling itself as a livable small city, offering tax advantages to business and "proximity to highways and rail routes" (see "Battling Rural 'Brain Drain,'" *Newsweek*, Dec. 26, 1988, 46). Effingham is thus following its tradition — at least 120 years old — of offering financial incentives in tandem with claims of locational advantages.

Exemplary Court Decisions

Four more exemplary state and U.S. Supreme Court decisions weave these strands together and provide concrete instances. The failure of small Illinois municipalities to pay their creditors precipitated all four cases, which are drawn from the list of municipal defaults compiled by Arthur Hillhouse (1935). They all show that the legal vulnerability of municipal government in the late nineteenth century was both more complex and less contested than the view through John Dillon's *Treatise on the Law of Municipal Corporations* might suggest. The cases rest on Illinois's 1870 constitutional limitation on the borrowing powers of local government, a limitation approved by the vast majority of those voting on the new constitution. They make it clear that although limited, the power of local government was still quite broad and that local governments vigorously pursued fiscal opportunities, often with the support of the courts and constitutions. We learn from these four examples that in essence local governments entered into forbidden and illegal debt obligations, paid their creditors reliably, and only years later used the illegality of the original obligation as a pretext for default. Logically, there may have been numerous illegal debts like these that were never contested because the cities consistently paid the creditors.

There is a separate legal and professional history that branches from cases just such as the ones discussed here. This is the rise of specialized bond counsel, attorneys whose responsibility and semipublic role has grown since the late nineteenth century. The current position is that such counsel has a special obligation to *all* parties concerned to assure that the debt is as stated; their role should be likened to that of a CPA. In addition, one theorist now contends that the burden of responsibility should flow to the entity in the "superior position," that is, the most knowledgeable party in the situation (Amdursky and Gillette 1992, 290–96).

In *Bissell et al. v. City of Kankakee* (1872), the Illinois Supreme Court affirmed a lower-court decision that Kankakee had never had the authority to borrow $500 to donate to the Douglas Linen Company, and that the debt was therefore not collectible. Kankakee (45 miles south of Chicago) was not the loser in this case, however, for the real issue was that the linen company had failed to perform. Its new mill had burned down on the day it was to open, resulting in a $30,000 loss (*Fulton County Ledger*, January 31, 1868, 2). The city then gave the company money to help it rebuild the mill. Apparently the mill never opened, so the city simply refused to repay its creditors. Had the unconstitutional loan helped in getting the

Douglas Linen Company off the ground, the city would presumably have repaid the debt gladly. A case that on the surface seemed to affirm the limited power of government actually thus helped a small city escape its promise to pay. Such sharp dealing was not limited only to small loans, as the following case illustrates.

In 1873, Litchfield, in the center of the state, exceeded the 5 percent debt limit of the 1870 constitution when it issued voter-approved bonds to build a waterworks. In 1880, the U.S. Supreme Court, in *Buchanan v. Litchfield*, supported the city in its refusal to repay the bonds, saying that they had exceeded the city's authority and therefore were not valid. But Litchfield's default did not come solely from either fiscal stress or a more deeply held conception of limited local government. Rather, it arose from complex local fiscal politics, led by an " 'anti-water-works party' " or anti-Republican " 'Ring,' " according to the *Litchfield Monitor*, the masthead of which proudly proclaimed itself "A Republican Journal Devoted to Home Interests" (April 6, 1878, 1). In fact, the incumbent city treasurer won the election of 1878 by default, as no one else would stand for the position, defeating the "ring." Less partisan than it would seem at first, the waterworks was the center of intense personal disputes, as were subsequent local elections in which parties did not endorse candidates. An increase in taxes precipitated the factional and personal political contests that developed two years after the original $50,000 was borrowed. Coming in the midst of a depression, these taxes had been resisted, and voters supported the repudiationist mayoral candidate. This strange local antagonism gives no real clue to the town's actual willingness to use debt responsibly, because in the mid 1880s, town voters overwhelmingly voted to tax themselves to fund a school debt (691 to 136 against) (*Litchfield Monitor*, April 11, 1885, 1). The court's decision, therefore, simply enforced one side of this local political/economic conflict.

In an 1882 decision, *Ottawa v. Carey*, the issue centered on the legality of a $60,000 city loan to a private water-power company. The city of Ottawa (about 50 miles southwest of Chicago) had intended the money to encourage a company planning to harness the Fox River's power. The power supply would in turn attract manufacturers, thus building this sector of the local economy.[7] A lawyer drew out this promotional intention clearly, when he asked a former council member in court, "Mr. Osman, was it your opinion that if these works were built and the machinery set in motion and [unclear in manuscript, but could be Mr. Cushman's] contract carried out fully, that the benefit to the community would be more than equivalent to the amount of these bonds?" Osman answered, "Certainly." He would not, however, commit himself as to the intentions of others:

Q: "Was that the general opinion of the conservative business men at the time the bonds were issued by this city?"
   A: "That, I can't say. I don't know what the conservative business men thought about it." (Illinois State Archives 140/287)

The poorly constructed water project failed to produce power: a flood in either 1872 or 1873 ruined what little had been built. The city refused principal and interest payments, and the bondholders sued to get their money back. The court ruled in favor of the city, agreeing with it that it did not have the power to do what it had done. The *Ottawa Republican* likened the decision to a "kick in the U.S. Supreme Court" (January 10, 1882, 1). The decision explicitly rested on Dillon's highly restrictive opinion that municipal corporations have no implied powers (108 U.S. 121). Cities' fiscal activities were limited, according to the court, to "corporate purposes." Admitting that such were difficult to decide, the court asserted that corporate purposes include only "expressly granted" powers. Chief Justice Waite stated quite bluntly of municipal corporations that "beyond their corporate powers their acts are of no effect."[8] The bondholders did not give up easily, and a few years later Louise Eames Mather, the niece of one of the original promoters and investors, also sued for her share of the debt. The Illinois Supreme Court this time agreed that the city had had no right to borrow the money in the first place. Justice Waite, in this as in other municipal debt cases, enunciated the principles first expressed by Dillon in his *Treatise on the Law of Municipal Corporations*. Said Waite: "Municipal corporations are created to aid the State government in the regulation and administration of local affairs. . . . No powers can be implied except such as are essential to the objects and purposes of the corporation as created and established."[9] Justice Waite thus made clear in principle as well as in fact, in this as in many other cases, that U.S. city governments enjoy a subsidiary position under the constraining dictates of John Dillon.

But the reason Ottawa had quit making payments had nothing to do with constitutional theory. From the city's point of view, the company had not performed: it had cheated Ottawa. When the city refused payment on the bonds, which the company had resold to persons fully familiar with the situation, it in effect stopped payment on a defective product. As in Kankakee, had the water-power scheme worked, the additional tax burden imposed by repaying bonds would have been acceptable to the voters of the town, and the courts would never have heard of any of these debts or the local promotional activities that caused them.

One might guess that a small city like Ottawa, so aggressive in its use of its borrowing capacity, would have been against the 1870 constitutional limitation of local debt. Not so, for Ottawa's clear, if cynical, use of local debt for development had not deterred it or its newspaper from supporting the debt-limitation section of the constitution. An editorial argued that "towns, counties and cities are voting away hundreds of thousands of dollars to irresponsible paper railroad companies, and even to private manufacturing establishments[, which] is fast becoming a matter of grave concern and alarm amongst thinking men. . . . The aggressive and all absorbing power of chartered monopolies already threatens the very existence of our civil liberties and political institutions" (*Ottawa Republican*, March 10, 1870, 4).[10] In these statements we see a subtle conception of local government power: recognition and exploitation of debt-issuing power went hand in hand with a concern that this power not be used beyond some unspecified but genuine limit.

Just as Ottawa had not been able to get the water power it wanted, or Kankakee its linen company, Aurora (35 miles due west of Chicago) could not get a railroad company to locate its general offices and machine shops in town. So it joined the same aggressive company of defaulters. In 1867, its voters had approved a donation of $50,000 to the Chicago, Burlington and Quincy Railroad Company to help it build its machine shops in town. The bonds were to be paid by a special assessment on the ward in which the shops were built, but the legislature failed to approve this special tax by the time the town issued the debt. Aurora then refused to pay the principal and interest to the bondholders, claiming that the conditions of the original bonds had not been fulfilled. The legal case hinged on this technical question. It is clear that the city's goodwill toward the bondholders would have been different had the railroad also located its general offices in Aurora, which the city had "understood" its president "proposed to do when the aid was voted him" (the Republican *Aurora Beacon*, July 22, 1881, 1). The Illinois Supreme court, in *Chicago, Burlington and Quincy Railroad Co. v. City of Aurora*, agreed with the city that its bonds were not valid and that it did not have to pay the bondholders.

As opposed to Ottawa, whose residents complained of their high taxes, Aurora was well-off; at the time of its default, the city was debating the exciting question of how to spend a windfall $100,000 generated by the sale of its Chicago and Iowa Railroad stock. The *Aurora Beacon* discussed such options as new bridges, "a grand town public library," a "magnificent town hall . . . that would accommodate two thousand people on election day and at popular entertainments," a waterworks, a loan to a railroad, or, finally, a proposal to lend the money "to manufacturing enterprises at very small interest, and on good security" (July 22, 1881, 1), rather than using the money to liquidate the city's debt, even that for which it accepted responsibility. Essentially the court had helped a prosperous city renege on a promise to pay. The city, on the other hand, had expected the loan to be self-repaid and was also angry at the railroad company's lack of commitment. The city used a minor condition in the original bond issue to default, to punish the railroad's specific investment failure and to enhance its fiscal position. It had in no way been constrained in its borrowing.

These defaults corroborate the notion that, in general, the determination of defaults was political, not fiscal. Moreover, they make it clear that repudiation of a particular debt was not a rejection of the idea of debt in general, or of the principle of using debt for developmental purposes. In three of these cases, repudiation came as a form of retaliation against the aided enterprises, which locals felt had not lived up to their original agreements. What is unclear is the courts' understanding of the municipalities' positions: Did they actually think they were limiting local fiscal power when they helped a municipality escape an unfair burden? Did the courts see themselves as making a reality of Dillon's principles?

In all four cases, the evidence is overwhelming that if the aided enterprises had pleased the towns in their performance, more money (possibly illegally obtained) rather than repudiation would have been forthcoming. No doubt these cases did not deter future lenders who had confidence in particular assisted enterprises. And in the case of debt issued illegally, the illegality of the debt only became a meaningful issue if and when the town defaulted. We have no way of knowing how much excessive debt or debt for unconstitutional purposes towns issued, for if they paid principal and interest, the courts would never hear about the matter. These cases suggest that the constitutional limitations on local debt ratified in 1870 served as a useful tool for towns in punishing nonperforming enterprises but may not have had the severe limiting effect we have mistakenly tended to read into them. Were there hundreds of municipalities borrowing beyond their debt limits but paying happy lenders? Such massive evasion seems highly improbable, but the point is that some evasion would have conformed to the spirit of local debt control — the idea was control, not abolition. And the rules of the financial game cities and towns played were in fact quite flexible and open to negotiation; in that game, the law was a backdrop, not a steel template.

The detailed narrative analysis in Chapter 5 of the local political circumstances and economic precipitants of several local default incidents, including those of Watertown, Wisconsin, Duluth, Minnesota, and Memphis, Tennessee, and the ensuing court battles — which in the case of Watertown went as far as the U.S. Supreme Court — demonstrates further that the defaults were political actions rather than purely economic reactions. These well-known (at the time) cases, which demonstrate the apparent willingness of local governments to default on their obligations if politically expedient, help us understand why state debt limits could later be interpreted as an attempt to force responsibility on local governments.

CHAPTER FIVE

The Politics of Spectacular Defaults

One thing is certain[;] the debt must be paid, sooner or later,
and the League organization must be seized with a bad attack
of hallucination if it ever hopes to avoid it. In the mean time
the city is growing, but if the debt was removed it would grow
still faster.

— *Watertown Democrat*, May 10, 1877

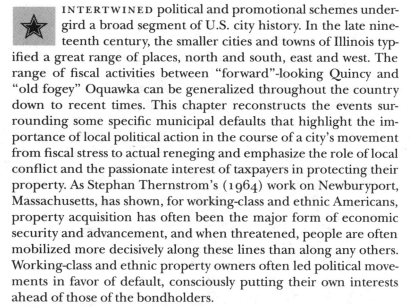 INTERTWINED political and promotional schemes under-
gird a broad segment of U.S. city history. In the late nine-
teenth century, the smaller cities and towns of Illinois typified a great range of places, north and south, east and west. The
range of fiscal activities between "forward"-looking Quincy and
"old fogey" Oquawka can be generalized throughout the country
down to recent times. This chapter reconstructs the events surrounding some specific municipal defaults that highlight the importance of local political action in the course of a city's movement
from fiscal stress to actual reneging and emphasize the role of local
conflict and the passionate interest of taxpayers in protecting their
property. As Stephan Thernstrom's (1964) work on Newburyport,
Massachusetts, has shown, for working-class and ethnic Americans,
property acquisition has often been the major form of economic
security and advancement, and when threatened, people are often
mobilized more decisively along these lines than along any others.
Working-class and ethnic property owners often led political movements in favor of default, consciously putting their own interests
ahead of those of the bondholders.

The challenge is to determine when political initiative cannot
work and in what ways external circumstances bound it. The major
defaults and economic prostration of Duluth, Memphis, and Watertown in the 1870s and 1880s, and of Detroit in the 1930s, recon-
firm the notion that until the Great Depression, the appropriate
context in which to locate defaults was not the fortune of the national economy. Rather, the entrepreneurial nature of the nine-

teenth-century city, collusion between state and local government, and, always most important, the dimensions of local political and economic struggles determined who defaulted and when. When we think of debt in relation to capital improvements of the infrastructure, improvements that increase a city's "service" capabilities in one way or another, we may forget how essential they are to the city's economic base. Nineteenth-century city officials knew this and knew that their governments acted more as economic innovators than as mere service providers. Debt underwrote and promoted their economic growth, attracted outside investment, and repaid the cities' inhabitants in rising property values. Whether buying a fire engine or building a railroad spur into town, the explicit purpose was to promote faster economic growth. And when the fire engine burned up, or the railroad never got built, taxpayers often chose to stop payment, particularly if the economic future of the whole town appeared to be in jeopardy. Lenders then had to threaten, plead, or sue for their money. For instance, both John Jacob Astor and Cornelius Van Schaack Roosevelt wrote letters to the city of Detroit pleading for overdue bond payments in 1844 and 1845 (Burton 1917, 154–55).

When events came to this pass, state and local governments frequently colluded against the debt holders' interests. Legislators quickly voted cities out of existence to frustrate repayment or lawsuits, while hair-splitting judges helped cities avoid their legal obligations. If city officials foolishly tried to make interest or principal payments during a financially troubled time, the townspeople themselves became activists in the cause of nonpayment, sometimes threatening violent retribution against those who advocated repayment. In the midst of all this the pleas of the bondholders fell upon a succession of deaf ears.

The default case studies in this chapter are more than local morality plays, however. Each has been selected from a period of high default activity. Within this framework, each case has been analyzed because of its more extensive documentation, usually a by-product of its sensational nature. For the era prior to the wholesale reneging of 1933, newspapers have been searched for further details of these local defaults. The greater visibility of these cases may perhaps introduce bias: cases that received less public attention may have had different causal structures. The cases analyzed in Chapter 4 should provide a corrective perspective, however, and the fact is that even the most exciting of these cases, that of Watertown, did not generate front-page news (except, of course, in the defaulting city). Rather than searching for villains and victims, the case studies present a further sampling of the responses of cities to fiscal crisis in the nineteenth and early twentieth centuries. The individual default scenarios analyzed in this chapter have been selected to represent cases from the major time periods of default and to illustrate the most extreme, even sensational, defaults. In Duluth and Memphis default was apparently the result of a catastrophe: the economic collapse of a large single employer in Duluth and epidemic disease in Memphis. From a purely fiscal perspective, the two causes had seemingly similar effects: rapid depopulation, followed by property tax delinquencies. The sudden failure of great numbers of people to pay property taxes enormously increased the tax burden on the cities' surviving property holders, virtually forcing defaults. Yet closer examination shows that the cases differ significantly: the default of Memphis masked a virtual coup d'état, similar to political takeovers in other southern cities during the Gilded Age.[1]

The other two cases analyzed in this chapter, those of Watertown, Wisconsin, and Detroit, constituted somewhat different situations. The failure of a railroad company precipitated Watertown's sensational and deliberate default. Several aspects of the case make it an instructive, legally definitive example. Sharply drawn class and ethnic conflict swirled through various political organizations precipitated by intense local political activity during the city's two decades of default, and contemporary newspapers record some of the sophisticated and articulate dialogue exchanged. Moreover, the Watertown crisis received nationwide publicity because of concurrent state legislative and federal supreme court actions.

Detroit's default achieved instant national prominence for several reasons that had nothing to do with the local circumstances of the default itself. Unlike the other cities analyzed in this chapter, Detroit apparently had no choice but default, and probably only intervention by the federal government or someone like Henry Ford could have staved it off. The national impact of the default was unprecedented because the city stood for the most positive aspects of American urban politics and economics. Detroit was the fourth-largest city in the United States. It symbolized the progressive technology of the automobile. In Frank Murphy it had a nationally prominent and politically progressive mayor. If Detroit could not meet its obligations, no city was invulnerable.

Duluth, 1870–1887

Today Duluth no longer even figures in the *New York Times* weather list; only the *Los Angeles Times* retains it, presumably to send shivers down the spines of comfortable Southern Californians. And when the city does make the news, it is for toxic spills, for repentance over its past sins (a vicious triple lynching in 1920), or as a source of humor (as in Gore Vidal's novel *Duluth!* or the 1993 journal article "Take Duluth . . . Please") or a booster's platform (as in a 1991 article in *Public Management* on the city's "revival").[2] Colonel Sellers, the antihero of Mark Twain's *The Gilded Age* (1873), would have had a field day promoting Duluth, for unlike Napoleon, it had Lake Superior for a waterway to the east. Yet, as in Goose Run, some improvements were necessary before it could take its rightful place in the universe. In fact, one of its early promoters sounds as if he had taken his language directly from Twain: "Oh, it was fun starting and running a city in those days! Most of the citizens were busted when they came here and wanted to get rich quick and easy. Of course they were willing to work themselves and to work the other fellow at the same time. It was all a gamble, though Nature dealt some good cards along with the jokers" (Cooley 1925, 19).

The western city of the nineteenth century is best understood as a capitalist venture, founded with very little capital and much windy rhetoric.[3] The absurd promotional rhetoric boosting Duluth was ridiculed early in its history in an 1871 speech made to Congress by Proctor Knott of Kentucky. The speech was later published as a pamphlet titled simply *Duluth!* Knott belittled the request of a group of Wisconsin investors for a land grant to build a railroad across northern Wisconsin terminating at Superior, Duluth's even-less-promising "twin port." "Duluth!" Knott mocked. "The word fell upon my ear with peculiar and indescribable charm. . . . Duluth! Twas the name for which my soul had panted" (Woodbridge and

Pardee 1910, 351). Laughter punctuated Knott's speech, but his mockery of this proposed "commercial metropolis of the earth" did not deter the city's publicists (ibid., 357). Within two years of being made the butt of his congressional joke, the city's promoters pressed on, unconscious of the fatuousness of their rhetoric. *Duluth*, a booklet published in 1873 by H. T. Johns, typifies such rhetoric, extolling the prospects and virtues of Duluth. "A glance at the map will show," it begins in all seriousness, "that if nature ever designated any place for a great city, it is Duluth, Minnesota" (Johns 1873, 1).

At its founding, Duluth's existence was little more than legal fiction. The first European inhabitants of this small Ojibway fishing village all departed when the winter of 1857 arrived, fearing six months of ice-bound isolation. Yet a handful of people returned to promote investment in Duluth, which by 1860 had platted building sites for 40,000 people, although the actual white population hovered between 60 and 80. By 1870, the city boundaries enclosed 3,500 acres — more than an acre per resident.

In 1869, the financier Jay Cooke announced his grandiose plans for the great Northern Pacific Railroad, designating Duluth as its eastern terminus and port facility. Here the bounteous Dakota wheat harvests would be transferred to ships bound for the east and for the world. This commercial promise brought small-time entrepreneurs to what was chartered as the City of Duluth in March 1870. Duluth's entrepreneurs optimistically planned a major metropolis largely on the basis of Jay Cooke's speculative hopes. The active local agents in this venture saw themselves as members of a privileged club, in which families, women, blacks, Indians, and wage laborers all had very minor places. Indians, for instance, were either objects of humor or portrayed as barriers to the proper development of economic enterprises. "They are too much like mere animals to cultivate the fertile soil, mine the coal, develop the salt mines, bore the petroleum wells, or wash the gold," declared the *Yankton Dakotian* (quoted in the *Duluth Weekly Tribune*, September 10, 1874). These men's fraternal camaraderie rarely ruptured, and then only during recessions, when municipal debt enriched a few of the group's members, while hurting others.

A year after Cooke's plans to build Duluth had been announced, the city's population had grown to at least 2,500. And five months after receiving its city charter, the city had successfully issued $50,000 worth of bonded indebtedness. These early bonds exemplify the creative, entrepreneurial use of municipal debt. The Lake Superior and Mississippi Railroad terminated a frustrating one mile from the planned city center. "The citizens of Duluth got together in a sort of indignation meeting to see what they could do about it. The result was the city council ordering the issuing of $50,000 twenty-year bonds, drawing seven percent interest, in favor of the railroad company. Ostensibly to assist in defraying the expenses of digging the canal and putting in the piers [for the city's port facilities]; but really as a bonus to the company to get them started to extend their line as far as Fifth Avenue East" (Cooley 1925, 16).

For the first three years of the city's corporate life, the optimism of its elite ballooned with the city's debts, one early participant claiming that bonds were issued for anything that could be imagined. Any resistance to debt issuance "would have been considered treason. It was as much as a man's life was worth, if he had even suggested caution" (Cooley 1925, 17). For instance, in April 1873, the city council proposed and the voters approved a bond issue of $30,000 to a Blast-Furnace Company. That the directorship of the council overlapped with the company's founders made little difference in the heady days of the boom. But after Jay Cooke and Company failed in September, and most employment ceased in Duluth, the payment of interest on these bonds suddenly seemed wrong and unfair to the handful of remaining urban residents. By 1874, the population of the city had fallen from an estimated 5,000 to 1,500, and the Duluth *Tribune* published long lists of tax-delinquent properties and owners. The paper had full columns of mortgage foreclosure sales. Tax revenues plummeted, and most of the remaining Duluthians wished to repudiate the city's bonded indebtedness.

Those few who wished to make interest payments on the bonds claimed they stood for good business principles and ethical behavior, while the repudiationists referred to them as a "ring" of bondholders trying to gouge money out of the city's stricken taxpayers. The panic in Duluth deepened into a depression, and while the repudiationists did not have their way directly, indirectly they did. With the assistance of the sympathetic state legislature, the City of Duluth disappeared, reformed as the "District of Duluth," which had no chief executive and therefore no responsible person to be sued. The District of Duluth enclosed about 40 percent of the area of the previous city, and as it redeemed the bonds at 25 cents on the dollar, it could purchase back the old city property.

Within six months of the creation of the District of Duluth, the legislature created the Village of Duluth, as succinctly stated in a circuit court case:

This act carved the village out of the city limits, taking and embracing in the village all the business part of the city and business houses, the harbor, railroad depots and tracks, nearly all the dwelling-houses, all the population except about 100 inhabitants, and nineteen-twentieths of all the taxable property: and no provision was made for the payment of the debts of the city by the village unless creditors would accede to the terms imposed by the legislature as hereinafter stated. It also appears that on February 28, 1877, an act was passed entitled "An act to amend the act to incorporate the city of Duluth," approved March 5, 1870, and this act declared that the service of all summons and process in suits against the city of Duluth should be made on the mayor of the city, and that service made on any other officer should not be valid against the city. It also provided that the term of the office of mayor should cease on the following April, 1877, and no provision was made for the election of a successor or for filling a vacancy; that no taxes should be levied without the affirmative vote of all, to-wit, four aldermen; and since the passage of the act there have never been four aldermen in the city qualified to act. (*Brewis v. City of Duluth,* 9 F. 747 [1881])

In *Brewis* the court reiterated a doctrine established in *Broughton v. Pensacola,* 93 U.S. 266 (1876), that succeeding municipal corporations became liable for all the debts of preceding corporations. Not until eleven years after the creation of the district and subsequent village did Duluth regain city status.

Both the conflict over debt repudiation and the final strategy to deal with the city's debt are revealing. The conflict essentially pitted the taxpaying property owners of the city against the more aggressive entrepreneurs, like the city council members who had created the Blast-Furnace Company and then capitalized it with city bonds.

The "ring" represented those men who had been able to lend the city some money. The resolution of the conflict represented a triumph of sorts for the uninvolved property holders. With the assistance of the state legislature, the redrawing of city boundary lines, and the dissolution of the debt-contracting entity called the "City of Duluth," municipal debt was dramatically diminished. This speculative frontier industrial city with little capital or infrastructure thus behaved like a private corporation, going bankrupt for all practical purposes, acquiring a court-appointed administrator to watch over its affairs as a "district," and paying off its debtors at 25 percent.

Issued on speculation that the city would indeed turn into something real, Duluth's debt encumbered only the handful of property owners who had too great a proportion of their resources sunk in it to be able to leave. The city's assessed property value fell by 50 percent between 1872 and 1874. The only people who had an interest in debt payment were the "ring of city bondholders" (*Duluth Weekly Tribune* February 28, 1874, 1).

The individual stances on debt repayment taken by property owners fell into one of two categories, depending on whether they stood to gain more from their bonds than they stood to lose in property taxes. This is one case where the citizens of the city really did not have that much more to lose by abandoning their property, as some apparently did, and leaving the remains to the city's creditors. The sleight of hand in the creation of the District and then Village of Duluth allowed the nucleus of the city to struggle along until prosperity returned, although as late as 1883, the chastened voters turned down a bond issue for construction of a city hall. City policy seems to have turned toward annexation of the forest surrounding Duluth, so that by 1895 its land area had expanded to ten times that of 1880. Its boundaries encompassed an area large enough to accommodate 400,000 people comfortably, according to the city engineer's calculation (Horwitz 1939, 7).

Watertown, Wisconsin

Watertown's debt-payment ordeal illustrates another extreme dimension of urban financing. It prompted a writer in the *North Amer-*

ican Review to ask, "Are we a nation of rascals?" (Hume 1884, 127). Compared to Duluth, Watertown was well-off. But because of its huge debt load, the persistence of its creditors, and the complexity of its social, economic, and political structure, its nearly four-decade struggle over debt displays the complete range of local responses to an urban fiscal crisis.

In 1856, the Wisconsin legislature authorized the issuance of $400,000 in bonded debt by the city of Watertown to aid railroads (Whyte 1916, 273). These bonds were divided between two fledgling railroads, which were apparently both to repay the principal and make interest payments. Such an arrangement was in effect a collateralization, the city's credit underwriting the railroad's capitalization. The panic of 1857 caused one of the railroads to collapse, and the lessees of the company sold the city's bonds in Boston for 32.5 percent of their face value (Whyte 1916, 277). The other, the Milwaukee and St. Paul Railroad, traded its stock to Watertown for city bonds, but the resulting $200,000 debt brought the city neither railroad nor capital improvements; rather, "its crushing weight stayed its growth [and] paralyzed its industries," according to William F. Whyte (1916, 278). By 1870, Watertown's debt, plus interest, equaled 50 percent of the city's property value.

Although in retrospect one may doubt whether Watertown's destined greatness was foiled by this debt, it is apparent that it became Watertown's dominating public and political issue. In 1867, townspeople met and discussed various schemes to deal with it, from proposals to buy up the discounted debt to "foolish speeches" in favor of repudiation (Whyte 1916, 281). By 1868, however, the city had discovered a more ingenious solution to its problem. It governed itself without officers upon whom legal papers could be served, beginning over two decades of governing without government. City business was always dealt with *before* the first council meeting, which was followed by a handing in of all signed business documents (e.g., motions made and approved) and resignations to the city clerk. City management was handled by the Board of Street Commissioners, whose regular order of business in 1874, for example, included paying city employees and allocating money from a "poor fund" for medical assistance to a poor woman (Watertown *Democrat*, September 10, 1874). Two years later, in 1876, at its regular meeting, the Board of Street Commissioners planned the upcoming Fourth of July celebration, arranging prizes and processions and stipulating that school children would sing patriotic songs (ibid., March 9, 1876).

The courts awarded one judgment and then another against Watertown, but creditors found no one on whom to serve papers. Then, in 1872, the Wisconsin state legislature passed a bill making it impossible to seize private property to satisfy municipal creditors, effectively protecting the city's property owners.

The Watertown *Republican* (March 6, 1872) alleged that the city's debt had been issued irresponsibly by the propertyless, "by a rabble of railroad laborers thrown out of employment on a road that had stopped." These propertyless workers encumbered honest property owners, including, of course, "every widow and orphan" — who would gladly pay a real debt, but refused "to satisfy the avarice of the men . . . who have combined to use the wealth they wrung from the sweat and blood of the farmers of Wisconsin [referring to the great mortgage scandals of the 1850s] to buy these Railroad bonds against cities, towns, counties, and villages, at a small fraction of their par value, in order to build their fortunes upon the ruin of so many." The editorialist continued to threaten a revolution of decent townspeople if the greedy speculators persisted.

In an incident remarkably similar to the Captain Swing riots forty years earlier in England (Hobsbawm and Rude 1975), five of the town's "prominent and influential citizens" (including two former mayors) awoke one summer morning in 1872 to find miniature wooden coffins on their doorsteps. Letters with the coffins urged: "In this bury all your Railway Bonds and your villainy with it. Beware!" (Watertown *Republican*, June 26, 1872).

A month later the pro-repudiation forces formed an organization of working-class homeowners, the Union League, which was to play an influential role in city politics for the next two decades. Led by a man named Patrick Devy, this bilingual, German-Irish Democratic organization continued to be active in Watertown until 1897. The League's secret Committee of Safety agitated against all bond payments and threatened to burn down the city if creditors tried to collect the debt or seize private property to pay it.

The Union League saw the debt as a plot of the wealthy against the workers. (William F. Whyte wrote of "pestilent demagogues . . . raising the cry of class against class" [1916, 268–307]). G. Baumann told the League on September 14, in an address in both German and English, that "a certain clique of cunning men . . . men who from the first setting of this place had subsisted on the sweat of the laboring class of Watertown" had foisted the debt on the town. Their plot was foiled and resisted by the "workingmen only who fight for Right and Home" (Watertown *Republican*, September 18, 1872). The anti-repudiation *Democrat* called the League's meetings a " 'hodge-podge mess of drivelling, drooling gibberish and contemptible bosh' " (January 2, 1873; quoted in Whyte 1916, 297).

The League's vigorously militant and threatening utterances show little visible drivel, and by September it had passed a unanimous resolution in German and English that gives a sense of the depth of its members' passion. "Resolved that the Union League of the City of Watertown will use all justifiable means to protect their property from legal robbers as they would from thieves and highway robbers" (Watertown *Republican*, September 4, 1872). Meanwhile, an ineffective Citizens' Association, formed in opposition to the League, worked to compromise the debt in some way. The League's political power grew, as first Devy and then Hezekiah Flinn, another Leaguer, gained legislative seats in the late 1870s, where they worked to keep the debt unpaid.

The bondholders persisted in their legal effort at recovery. The Supreme Court, in *Amy v. Watertown* (130 U.S. 301 [1889]; Amy is sometimes spelled Almy), ruled that the debt must be served on the mayor, and that the state legislation's prescribing of this mode of service was proper. That the mayor was never present could not be brought into the argument. This case effectively sealed Watertown's deadlock with the bondholders. The Milwaukee attorney who had represented the bondholders for 25 years, and perhaps held most of the bonds himself, then settled with the city, turning over $600,000 worth of bonds for $15,000. In 1894, the city government began "normal" operations again, thus ending 35 years of turmoil.

The numerous local groups complicate Watertown's story. Townspeople took five different positions. The handful of well-off local capitalists who also held city bonds wanted complete payment of the debt. Out-of-work railroad laborers supported the original debt, but whether they later joined the repudiation groups or moved on is not clear. The Union League—German, Irish, and Democratic—although not in tune with the town's democratic newspaper, advocated strict repudiation but also seemed to represent the numerous small property holders as well as the propertyless. The Citizens' Association, apparently Republican, wanted to compromise the debt, a position comfortable to the smaller entrepreneurs and probably to all three town newspapers. And finally, non-League Democrats maintained an uneasy fifth position that skirted around favoring complete repudiation.

That property owners so militantly supported the anti-establishment Union League is no surprise, for as in Duluth and most newly founded western cities, the acquisition of small real property holdings was possible for all but the totally destitute (Underwood 1982). Economic class differences grew at the margins between (1) these very small property owners, who could literally tear down their houses and move them to another town, (2) the local entrepreneurs who possessed a bit of capital and the spirit typified by the Duluthian who happily worked hard but "worked the other fellow at the same time," and (3) the handful of local capitalists who invested heavily in city bonds and local business in addition to their regional activities. These three economic classes were fractured by splits of ethnicity, articulated as political party divisions.

The class locations of the actors in part determined their various positions on debt. Small property holders willingly issued debt and willingly repudiated, standing to gain from debt but having little to lose from default. Petty capitalists who had tied their economic future to that of the city supported the issuing of debt because it promised growth, and to preserve its good credit, they favored debt payment when feasible and renegotiation when not. The few wealthy resident bondholders and backers of larger corporate local enterprises (like the Blast-Furnace Company in Duluth, for example) wanted debt payment at all costs. Partisan politics and ethnicity reshaded these basic positions. Watertown's Democrats and its Irish voters, who might have favored repudiation were they in the post-Reconstruction South, fragmented in their analyses of their immediate economic interests. Republicans, "Americans of the New England Puritan type, men of refinement and culture" (Whyte 1916,

285), the native-born, and some Germans would in general work for the soundness of the city's credit and "reputation."

Although quite different in local circumstances and forms of political mobilization, Duluth and Watertown resembled one another in key ways. Both cities issued debt to foster economic growth, and in both cities political conflict occurred when that growth did not reach expectations. This sequence of events differed from those in Memphis and Detroit. In Memphis, fiscal problems became caught up in a struggle for municipal political power; in Detroit, the city's problems were beyond the control of any group or faction.

Memphis

If Duluth and Watertown were something less than solid, secure cities when they defaulted, the same cannot be said of Memphis, which was a relatively well-established cotton and commercial center of 40,000 in the 1870s. Memphis contained a rough and vigorous ethnic population in addition to its economically powerful commercial elite, and its fiscal policies were as risk-averse as Duluth and Watertown's were risk-oriented. It provided urban services reluctantly and tolerated ethnic voters grudgingly. Devastated in 1878 by a yellow fever epidemic that killed about 5,000 of its 40,000 population, Memphis faced an immediate problem in tax collection. The "solution" to this problem came when the Tennessee legislature reorganized the city as the "Taxing District of Shelby County" in 1879, a form that persisted until 1891. Mobile, Alabama, followed suit in 1879, Selma in 1884, and in 1915, Nashville, Tennessee, also went into receivership. Although simultaneously considered a mode of debt repudiation, the Taxing District made the installment payment of back taxes possible, and it repaid the city's debt, albeit at a reduced rate that averaged about 50 percent (Hillhouse 1935, 60).

Memphis thus appears to illustrate an early instance of state intervention. The "Taxing District" put the city into a virtual receivership. Commissioners actually governed the city, decades before voters ratified the nominally progressive commission structure in 1910. The state's handling of the crisis was proposed as a model for a "progressive" solution to local fiscal failure in the 1930s. Sim-

eon E. Leland asserts, for instance, that the new government elimi-
nated the "old ward bosses who were largely responsible for the
plight of the city" (1932, 18). It also effectively disenfranchised
voters, however, and closer examination shows that the original
"fiscal" crisis was a political crisis, which the city's creditors and elite
sought to resolve by eliminating ethnic and black political power.

Historians of Memphis offer at least two dissimilar versions of the
city's default saga and government liquidation in 1879. The first is
ideological, embedded in the historiography of Reconstruction.
Radical Republicans and their dupes, the black voters, foisted mil-
lions of dollars in fraudulent debt on the city. When redeemed by
the Democrats in 1879, even fiscal caution could not save Memphis,
and it went under, the victim of "Reconstruction waste and corruption" (Sigafoos 1979, 53).

The second story is biological, and in it Memphis is likewise
portrayed as the victim of outside forces. The city would have grown
to its destiny as a southern economic trailblazer, but for the yellow
fever epidemics of 1878 and 1879 (Capers 1939, 200–213; Sigafoos 1979, 53–65; Sorrels 1970, 29–41). Wiping out over 10 percent of the population, the epidemics caused such demographic
and economic damage that Memphis collapsed. Had it not been for
the epidemics, Memphis historians often assert, the city would have
led Atlanta and St. Louis in size and importance (Capers 1939,
208–9). The repudiation of the state debt of Tennessee in the same
era should lead us to question the blaming of the Republicans or
yellow fever for the city's fiscal problems. Both versions of the story
need some examination, for underneath them lies a third explanation, one that shows the similarities of Memphis to Watertown and
indicates why Memphis did not collapse fiscally in the 1930s when
so many other cities did.

Reconstruction actually had little effect on the debt of Memphis
(Capers 1939, 170–74). Recently enfranchised black voters tipped
the city toward supporting the Republican gubernatorial candidate
in 1867, but local conservatives wooed the black vote sufficiently to
elect a conservative mayor in January 1868. The city thus never
actually had a Republican mayor during Reconstruction. The myth
of Republican irresponsibility is so strong, however, that Gerald
Capers, the historian most willing to accept the notion of a Radical

government, asserts that "the advent of the Radicals to power meant merely that two bands of thieves instead of one would pillage the public" (1939, 181).

When historians refer to Reconstruction government in Memphis, they actually mean very modest state and federal interference—for instance, the appointment by the governor of a state-controlled police commission. Of course, these "Radicals" had no control over bond issues, and much of the city's debt had been incurred prior to the allegedly "Radical" government. By 1860, for example, the city had issued a million dollars in railroad debt, over half of which proved unrecoverable (Capers 1939, 128–29).

The paucity of mortality data and information makes a thorough analysis of the Memphis yellow fever crises difficult, but there are some suggestive details. Capers indicates that more than 5,000 people died of yellow fever, over one-eighth of the city's population. In itself, he argues, this would have been a powerful precipitant of financial crisis. But he shows, too, that at least half of the victims were the very poor Irish immigrants; the native-born white elite simply abandoned the city during the summer, both in 1878 and 1879. Most of the Irish lived in a section of the city called Pinch, adjacent to the river and Bayou Gayoso, a swampy open sewer that performed the functions of Rome's Cloaca Maxima, but without any flushing system (Sigafoos 1979, 39–40, 56). Relatively few blacks appear to have died compared to the 50 percent Irish mortality rate. Clearly the city's population growth suffered drastically, declining from 40,230 in 1870 to 33,592 in 1880. On the other hand, the county as a whole grew slightly, from 76,378 in 1870 to 78,430 in 1880. Taking into account the city's share of the county population, it is evident that the county alone grew substantially, from 36,148 to 44,838. This suggests that were ward-level population figures available, an even more specific pattern of depopulation would appear. Because the Taxing District did not preserve the city's wards, an estimate of the ward-by-ward impact is too unreliable to use. Vital records for Tennessee only account for half the total estimates of mortality, so that estimating ethnic proportions from these records would also reflect unknown biases. Yellow fever did not so much devastate Memphis as devastate one part of Memphis and one group of Memphians, but further proof seems unavailable (Hughes 1969–71, 16–18).

Because the very poor whites were most heavily victimized by the disease, and because the city had an unusually low overall proportion of home ownership (only 29 percent in the 1920s) (Sigafoos 1979, 136), one must at least question the fiscal impact of yellow fever on tax payments. Capers argues that the disease drove many merchants away to St. Louis, but more recent work by Sigafoos finds only a handful of such cases. He argues that many left the city only temporarily, returning to their cotton factoring by winter (Capers 1939, 205–6; Sigafoos 1979, 63–65). Thus, although yellow fever destroyed the attraction of the city for immigrants, its overall economic impact appears to have been exaggerated.

Instead of these two external causes, the city's default and legal disappearance should be seen as a political solution to underlying economic and political problems, engineered by its commercial elite. The first economic problem was a failure to reduce the debt through the 1870s, so that it grew from $4 to $6 million between 1872 and 1878. The second came from tax defaults amounting to perhaps 50 percent by 1878. And the third and perhaps most basic underlying factor was the decrease in cotton-factorage incomes, which declined by one-third between 1870 and 1878. Debt thus increased, tax revenues decreased, and the city's principal form of mercantile income diminished.

The major political problem facing the merchant elite was the allegedly increased power in city government of propertyless voters, " 'a large and controlling voting element which has but little at stake in the welfare of our city' " (Capers 1939, 202). The default of the city was in fact a solution most favorable to its elite, which was struggling simultaneously for its economic existence and political control. In addition, default was a popular idea on the state level in this period (Sigafoos 1979, 53–54; and Appendix B). For instance, when he campaigned in Memphis in late November 1878, the winning gubernatorial candidate, Albert S. Marks, emphasized a negotiated debt compromise with the holders of state bonds (Jones 1977, 980). From 1873 until 1879, the representatives of the city's commercial elites had consistently striven to disenfranchise the propertyless and the poor. It took the Memphis Cotton Exchange, the Chamber of Commerce, and the People's Protective Association six years to remove city government from the hands of the voters (Capers 1939, 202–3). They had tried to do so by changing the city charter, going from ward-based to at-large elections. Switching to a commission form of government was clearly perceived by many voters, to quote one headline from 1875, as a " 'Bad Movement — Liberties of the People Endangered' " (Capers 1939, 263 n. 67). The debt and yellow fever crises thus constituted a problem for which the solution — seizure of political power by the city's elite — had been waiting (Keating 1886, 1: 623–43).

Although no direct evidence may be uncovered, most historians agree that Memphians hoped that through the state's creation of the Taxing District, the city would effectively repudiate its debt (Capers 1939, 211). The *New York Times* put it more bluntly when, on February 3, 1879, it called the plan an attempt " 'to enable Memphis to rob its creditors' " (Sigafoos 1979, 59). Operating as an early, if not the earliest, form of commission government, the Taxing District ended up both collecting back property taxes and paying the bondholders at a reduced rate. It ended ward-based politics but not corruption in the city, for after Memphis formally adopted a commission form of government in 1910, it became Boss E. H. Crump's territory for the next 45 years. By this account then, the disestablishment of the city government terminated the city's greatest period of electoral democracy and returned it to the hands of its commercial elite.[4]

The dissolution of Memphis and its replacement by a "taxing district" became important as a precedent in the South, most immediately for Mobile and Selma (see Clotfelter 1973, 33–49, on Memphis). The thoughtful discussion of it as a model by Simeon E. Leland in *Commerce*, a Chicago-based business magazine, emphasizes that three states had adopted a policy similar to Tennessee's in municipal receivership codes in 1931. Such codes were "distasteful but they are not to be classed as 'un-American,' " Leland argued (1932, 18). These codes all rescheduled debt payment or refunded the debt, basing the city's credit on reinvigorated efforts to collect back taxes and flexibility in easing their payment. All also disenfranchised the local voters, either completely or partially.

Once the Memphis merchant elite had firmly established itself, the city became more fiscally "responsible," thus confirming that this elite had earlier used the city's economic crisis for political, not fiscal, reasons. Memphis did not default in the Great Depression, although one might argue, based on its balance sheet alone, that the city had as much reason to do so, if not more, than did many defaulting jurisdictions (Sigafoos 1979, 165–72). However, unlike many cities in the Depression (Detroit, for example), Memphis did not aid its unemployed. Instead, it slashed expenditures, surviving with relative liquidity. Because of the city's low proportion of home ownership, fewer ordinary citizens exerted pressure to compromise the debt. And by the 1930s, its elite no longer wished to alienate New York bondholders.

Detroit

Detroit was a city where there was political consensus on the need to honor debt obligation. Conflict swirled around budget shares, around welfare, and around the size of the debt, but repudiation did not come up on any formal political platform. During the first three decades of the twentieth century, Americans perceived Detroit as a leader among cities for several reasons. A bastion of Progressive reform, the city stood for good government and planning. Its famous Progressive mayor, Hazen Pingree, had established a high standard of enlightened political leadership in the 1890s (Holli 1969). As the automobile industry expanded production, its products came to symbolize technological progress, while the Michigan economy and Detroit benefited. This political and economic importance attracted urban immigrants from abroad and within the United States, so that the city moved from thirteenth-largest to fourth-largest by the mid 1920s. Visiting Detroit in 1929, Matthew Josephson caught its spirit: it was "the most modern city in the world, the city of tomorrow." He saw Detroit's ebullient optimism reflected in a motto of Henry Ford's: "No American Boy Ever Became a Success by Saving Money." And he criticized the city from the humanistic perspective of Sinclair Lewis, arguing that its supersalesman mentality destroyed its soul, while materialism and greed led the citizens to turn their backs on pollution and urban blight (Josephson 1929, 243–78, excerpted in Holli 1976, 162–70).

Detroit aggressively expanded its territory to capture an expanding population, but Ford's location of his major production centers beyond city limits foreshadowed the impending divergence of its economic and political boundaries. Between 1905 and 1926, anticipating continued growth, the city multiplied its area almost fivefold through annexation. Its population matched this land expansion, growing slightly over five times between 1900 and 1930. In the Depression years, however, the city's population grew less than 4 percent, while its taxpayers had to bear the capital costs of the expansion into annexed territory (Conot 1974, frontispiece; Holli 1976, 269). Unfortunately for Detroit's financial future, the annexations missed many of the major industrial concentrations of the automobile industry, thereby losing much potential property tax income (Zunz 1982, 290–96).

Had the population and the automobile industry continued to expand, the city's annexation strategy would have paid off. But the costs incurred in providing urban services to these new areas anticipated increased property tax receipts, not a major depression. Of the total bonds issued between 1918 and 1929, 59 percent were for costs related to annexation: sewers, water, street railways, lighting, and annexations (Wengert 1939, table 2). The city issued 20 percent of this debt in 1921 alone. For the years 1917 to 1920, the average annual debt issued hovered at $5,500,000. As automobile manufacturing grew, the city watched the suburbs gain the new factories: Ford, particularly, made a specific effort to avoid city property taxes. Although suburbanization did not approach the rush of the 1960s and 1970s, it appeared to Detroiters that prosperity lay in capturing this population and industrial growth. Anticipating a rosy future if it abandoned its earlier, conservative course, the city therefore abruptly issued $54 million in debt in 1921, ten times the previous annual average (Wengert 1939, table 1).

By the end of the 1920s, as the consequences of massive suburban annexation and infrastructural expansion began to be felt, debt-service costs began to rise gradually, and they doubled in the fiscal year 1932–33. Simultaneously, tax collections declined after 1930, plunging almost 50 percent, from $64 million in 1930–31 to

$38 million by 1933–34. Large and small property owners alike defaulted on their tax payments. In 1927, less than 20 percent of the property tax revenue had been consumed by debt-service costs, but by fiscal year 1932–33, this proportion had soared to over 40 percent of the tax levy and a disastrous 66 percent of the amount actually collected (Wengert 1939, tables 3 and 14). Mayor Murphy tried to reduce the city's budget, but welfare demands soared, and one of the largest and most prosperous cities in the United States suddenly found itself in a desperate position. As mayor of America's most embattled city, Murphy became a focus of national attention (Gelfand 1975).

This balance sheet provides a local fiscal context for the city's default in 1933 and a concrete instance of the massive tumble into default of over 3,000 local governments in the early years of the Depression. Grim as things were in Detroit, a coalition of political, union, and business leaders worked toward meeting the welfare and debt demands on the city's budget. On behalf of the city, Murphy accepted the moral obligation to feed the starving, even though at least 25 percent of them were workers laid off from Ford's plant outside the city limits.[5] The unemployment crisis in Detroit was so terrible that it probably did produce starvation, but death registrations list only immediate cause, not etiology (for example, pneumonia, but not malnutrition).

In 1933, the very worst year for the city, Murphy actively organized mayors on the national level to appeal for more federal funds, dealt as best he could with a hostile state government, and desperately pared the city budget. One suspects Detroit might have survived without default had it not been for the more general, if temporary, economic collapse triggered by the state bank holiday in February.

By 1930, two bank holding companies — one controlled by General Motors, the other by Ford — did 87 percent of the banking in Detroit and over 50 percent of the state's banking. These banks had succeeded in propping up their slipping monetary positions by falsifying their accounts, but in February 1933, they could hold out no longer, and when Henry Ford refused to make them a loan (the first "Ford to City: Drop Dead"?), the bankers asked the governor to declare a bank holiday in order to avoid a panic. Some employers met this crisis by turning to out-of-state banks, but the city was unable to do so. It defaulted immediately on interest payments. People with cash cleaned out grocery stores, fearing famine. The city began to pay its employees in scrip (Conot 1974, 67–68).

The Michigan bank holiday precipitated a national bank holiday, forcing default on any city whose cash accounts could not cover payments due. In Detroit's case, the bank holiday functioned as a classic precipitant, making manifest a strong, but repressed, desire to default.

The account sketched thus far needs an additional element to make it complete. Detroit's citizens not only swelled the welfare rolls; they not only failed to pay 35 percent of their property taxes; they also participated in taxpayer demonstrations. Early in 1932, a coalition group calling itself the Associations for Tax Reduction combined the interests of real estate speculators who had invested heavily in new subdivisions and were unable to pay the taxes, much less sell the property, and unemployed and underemployed home-owners seeking tax relief. It sparked a petition drive to limit the city budget, thereby putting a lowered ceiling on property tax. The president of the organization was allegedly a professional realtor and speculator who was $150,000 in arrears on his taxes (Lunt 1965, 65).

The Associations for Tax Reduction portrayed itself as a leader in " 'the struggle of the taxpayer against the tax spender,' " and the evidence suggests that the movement was in fact a coalition repre-senting several diverse groups, ranging from the property specula-tors to smaller homeowners, who were indeed facing disaster. For instance, although the manager of the Associations for Tax Reduc-tion was a former member of the Detroit Real Estate Board, this group itself supported the mayor's campaign to defeat the budget-limitation proposal. In fact, business interests throughout the city all united behind the mayor to defeat the budget-limitation pro-posal, suggesting that those petitioning for tax reduction repre-sented just who they claimed they did, small property owners.[6]

As opposed to the earlier municipal defaults analyzed in this chapter, Detroit's was most clearly precipitated by a larger financial crisis, the closing of the banks. Yet the difference should not be overemphasized, for the elements of similarity are great. First, of course, came the city's aggressive infrastructural expansion, funded through large debt issues. This expansion was made in anticipation of continued and accelerated economic growth: in fact, one might argue that the city had not expanded quickly enough at the turn of the century. Second, this expansion enjoyed public support, as most of the bond issues were voted upon. Like the voters of Duluth and Watertown earlier, Detroit voters saw themselves as financing their own economic future. Third, when the larger economy faltered, the property tax payers wished to escape their prior obligation.

Unlike earlier tax protests during crises, the one in Detroit focused on the budget, and in so doing it called for the city government to determine the priorities for reducing expenditures. Additionally, the language of the tax-reduction movement was not so clearly anticapitalist and anti-bondholder as in the earlier movements. Consequently, historians have usually seen the movement as one composed primarily of real estate investors. Apparently the Associations for Tax Reduction cared only about taxes and would have been equally as happy had the city either ended welfare payments or defaulted on interest payments. The budget itself, not its purposes, began to occupy the singular focus of public attention. This seemingly minor shift signaled a new era of urban fiscal politics, a politics concentrating on a wholesale attack on the city services and the role of government.

With the exception of Detroit, then, the preceding case histories show how the apparent cycles of default between the 1850s and the end of the Great Depression arose from local political choices. Although Duluth, Watertown, Memphis, and Detroit indeed defaulted during national depressions that were causing great local fiscal stress, external economic forces solely did not force default on them. These case histories thus give specific support to the more general findings of the time-series analysis in Chapter 2, which identifies only one national default crisis, that during the Great Depression, as meaningful. And, Detroit's case makes it clear that the severe economic burdens imposed on the beleaguered city by the Depression did indeed overwhelm local initiative and response.

When combined with the aggregate-level statistical analysis, these four detailed case studies constitute a basis for several further generalizations. First, they show that urban fiscal crises can be more carefully separated into at least two basic categories: those that occur as a consequence of conscious local decisions (Duluth, Watertown, and Memphis) and those imposed by external circumstances (Detroit). Those determined by local actions can further be broken down into two subcategories, the first where political conflict drives fiscal policy (Watertown) and the second where fiscal policy masks political change (Memphis).

Additionally, analysis of these four cities' use and abuse of their debt-issuing powers sketches the transition from the ebullient, risk-taking, high-growth cities of the late nineteenth century to the more cautious, chastened cities of the late twentieth. We can readily see why conservative uses of city funds came to typify mature urban government: it helped assure political stability, a goal finally more important to city officials than adventurous growth.

Between the 1870s and the 1930s, the context of debt-based municipal finance shifted. Characteristically, nineteenth-century debt in growing cities underwrote a flamboyant variety of municipal investments, from factories to schools. The defaults of the period often arose out of local political conflict over the nature of growth, risk, and, ultimately, the precise role of city government. The very purposes of the debts themselves became the subject of public discourse. And when financial times got difficult, the public asked hard questions about who gained from the taxpayers' strain. On occasion, the consequences of this conflict resulted in purposeful and deliberate defaults sanctioned by partisan voters. As a long-run, secondary outcome, potentially controversial investments by cities declined. School bonds, not direct aid to private enterprise, became the safe investment. Neither Duluth nor Watertown were to invest again so directly in transport or industry. More cautious, less risky, incremental behavior came into vogue.

The defaults of Duluth and Watertown show how local class, political, and ethnic conflict could take the city budget as a rallying point for action. In the case of Watertown, this occupied no passing moment, but a whole generation's political struggle. In the case of Memphis, on the other hand, an economic and demographic crisis provided the opportunity for one of several political and economic factions to take over the workings of government. That Memphis met its debt payments during the much more devastating Depression of the 1930s suggests the extent to which subjective and political, not objective and fiscal, circumstances had prompted the city's earlier default. The central conflict distinguishing Memphis from the other cities examined in this chapter was not over what fiscal action to take, but over who should take it.

Subsequent defaults occurred over more banal, less controversial types of investments. As early as the 1880s, Memphis had given a hint of things to come, and by the 1930s Detroit more clearly demonstrated that the nature of indebtedness itself was no longer to be an issue. Instead, the ostensibly objective problem of meeting payment schedules occupied center stage. Detroit's default illustrates how fiscal crisis ultimately subsumed political conflict. The question of debt default in Detroit did not arise until the statewide banking crisis milked the city of its cash. When it did, service costs ranging from welfare expenditures to teachers' salaries all figured in the political rhetoric, but the essential precipitant of the default came from outside, as it were. The real controversy had begun to shape itself over the fact that the city spent money at all, not over how or why it did so.

Conclusion

FEDERALISM AND URBANISM

EVEN TWAIN'S Colonel Sellers, the bombastic promoter of the "metropolis" of Stone's Landing, had to admit, "It's in the rough yet, in the rough." And, probably, Stone's Landing, like many other imagined cities — Sumner, Kansas, for instance — never really happened. Although many of the nineteenth century's speculative towns disappeared, many, many more have replaced them. The city-building strategies that offended economic morality in the late nineteenth century by lending publicly borrowed money to private enterprise actually worked. In his easy and accurate lampoon of promoters, Twain was careful to differentiate between the sincere and the insincere, for he had seen town building transform the United States.

During the twentieth century, the nation's fundamental pattern of settlement has reversed. In the pivotal year 1920, half the population officially became urban (that is, lived in places with over 2,500 inhabitants). But becoming urban did not mean becoming dominated by metropolises. Only a decade after the United States had hit the 50 percent urban mark, the mean size of all cities over 2,500 actually began to turn down (Figure 13). This downturn was not only an artifact of the Great Depression, as it must have seemed then, for it has continued. Americans have rejected the large city for the small one, often, but not always, in a suburban locale. Other problems within cities, especially, but not only, the larger ones, have paralleled such moves. Many Stone's Landings have since turned into cities (five have even called themselves Napoleon, Colonel Seller's preferred name). But the transforming events of 1930–

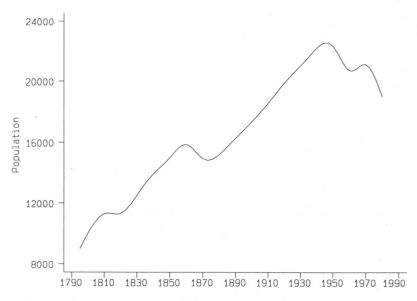

Figure 13. Mean city size in the U.S. (of places with population greater than 2,500), 1790–1990. Sources: Calculated from *Historical Statistics of the United States, Colonial Times to 1970, Bicentennial Edition* (Washington, D.C.: USGPO, 1975) and *Statistical Abstract of the United States* (Washington, D.C.: USGPO, various dates).

45, followed by the relative fiscal prosperity of the 1950s and 1960s, made the old problems of urban fiscal crisis seem new when they reappeared in the 1970s.

Since the mid 1970s, city fiscal problems have worried many Americans. Whether conceptualized as excess expenditures and excess taxes or inadequate revenues and failing services, no politician can either ignore or resolve the resulting stresses. These problems have, in turn, become metaphors for equally baffling social and infrastructural problems. Bridges fall down; sewage burbles up. The mentally ill wander the streets; families beg. As the twentieth century draws toward its conclusion, the prospect of an impending collapse of their cities is never far from urbanites' thoughts.

Any reader of this book knows that such fears and prospects are not new phenomena. But few urban policymakers remember, if they ever knew, that such was the nature of the American city at the time of the Civil War. Homeless children wandered the streets then, and even as early as the 1830s, untold thousands of them supported themselves. Every big city had newsboys' lodging houses where children could pay for a night's stay. Horatio Alger wrote dozens of popular novels about virtuous, self-supporting homeless children. One of his most famous heroes, Ragged Dick, boasted that he lived in "Box Hotel," referring to his packing case. The poor were not the only desperate urbanites: John Jacob Astor begged Detroit to repay him his loans in 1844, only a few years after its first city charter had been granted. Virtually from their modern beginnings, the specter of both fiscal and social collapse has haunted our cities.

Even as many cities teeter on the brink of disintegration, they exuberantly court growth and renewal, vigorously using their local tax resources.[1] From Memphis to Duluth, Quincy to New York, from 1830 down to the present day, cities have worked with energy and some craftiness to bring in tax-paying businesses and lower residential property taxes. Because this larger pattern has been played out in thousands of smaller dramas, it has made little impact on the more broadly drawn pages of history: little impact, that is, until confrontation flares. And when this happens, each new confrontation appears to be a sharp and surprising event. But in fact, such crises, sporadic, dramatic, and usually resolved, if not dissolved, have been central elements of American urban history ever since states granted cities their first charters.

The historical transformation of the United States from rural to urban paralleled an underlying metamorphosis of the American state structure. It is significant that the transformed institutions still retain elements of their origins, resulting in a political system of local governments uniquely dispersed across the political and geographical landscape, especially when compared with those of other Western nations. This dispersal has impeded clear historical description and analysis, which almost inevitably attends centralized federal programs but misses the complex, uneven web of local institutions.

Since World War II our cities, towns, and counties have lost their visible demarcations. Their populations and structures blur together. Even the Bureau of the Census prefers to report populations by "metropolitan areas," socially and visually logical units that embrace multiple and politically illogical governments. "Los Angeles," for instance, can refer to an enormous county of about ten million people or a city of four million that covers only about one-third of that county. Nearly a million "Angelenos" live in unincorporated Los Angeles County, which is urban to the eye; and there are nearly 90 other cities in the county, at least one of which, Long Beach, can hardly be conceptualized as "Los Angeles." Whether from the air or on the ground, it takes an expert to tell them apart. But at law, in the federal system, they are quite distinct.

It has become easy to forget that we live in a federal state; that the logic of federalism, embodied in the Constitution, structures the nature of all our government. The Constitution of the United States says nothing about cities, thus leaving their political and legal status to state governments. Given English precedents, the constitutional silence is predictable. The American War of Independence preceded Britain's rationalization of local government by sixty years. Urbanizing a hundred years before the United States, England fundamentally reshaped the local/central government relationship in the nineteenth century. The systematic and centralized structuring of English local government took its modern form in 1835, when the Municipal Corporations Act regularized municipal charters and brought them into final conformance with the will of Parliament. This, incidentally, accounts for the legal differences between local government in Canada and the United States; when Canada achieved its independent status, the Municipal Corporations Act had had three decades to be tested in England. Meanwhile, the United States had followed its own increasingly separate and very different path. The royal charters that undergirded some U.S. cities persisted into the nineteenth century, but they were then replaced by charters akin to those of private corporations. The age of corporate growth, usually associated with private enterprise, thus included municipal corporations in the United States.

State power seems to have percolated constantly upward or toward the center in our two centuries of constitutional government. This movement from the local toward the state, and then the federal, has helped create a kind of historical myopia. We look at the past from our understanding of the present, and as the present is so much more federalized, we tend to see only our federal past. This in turn reinforces our current federal consciousness, so that there is a constant strengthening of our centralized vision of the United States.

The contrasting sequence for the state and its institutions is worth summarizing in an imaginary time line.[2] The first period of the modern American state structure (1789–1830) saw the perfection of passive power: the quintessential action was the Supreme Court's assertion of power in *Marbury v. Madison* (1803). By the maneuver of saying it had the power to decide the case but not to enforce it, the court averted a potentially fatal power struggle with the president, asserted its right to judicial review, and defined its field of action. The Supreme Court thus lost the battle but won the war.

States in this period used corporate charters to accomplish actions for the public good through the granting of monopolies. Local governments and private charities, often subsidized by local governments, did the institution building in this period, with the exception of state institutions for housing felons and people with incurable disabilities. Virtually all of the ideas for these institutions originated at the city level.

In the second period of governmental innovation (1840–90), American states fostered corporate fiscal power, while the federal government freed corporations from state interference. In several rulings in the 1830s and 1840s, the Supreme Court freed corporations to do business anywhere in the United States, and later in the century it forestalled state-level efforts at corporate regulation (in the Granger cases, for instance). Economic enterprises sought grants and loans of money and credit from local governments, with outright federal land grants supplementing a few major railroads (like the Illinois Central). While state governments often shed bureaucracies involved in economic promotion and shunted off fiscal activity to local governments (Gunn 1988), they at the same time made major infrastructural investments in carceral institutions, from juvenile reform schools to elegant-looking prisons. This architectural heritage is still with us. By the end of this period, the state's visible presence was in control, care, and courts. Yet its fiscal presence underwrote wide-ranging economic enterprises.

In the third period (1890–1935), the federal state worked uneasily toward its current regulatory and bureaucratic form (Skowronek 1982; Karl 1983). The changes begun in the 1870s had slowly moved local government out of the business of subsidizing railroads. Through their boards of charities and corrections, state governments took a definite lead in welfare, broadly construed, consciously trying to remove it from local purview. County governments absorbed many urban relief functions, all under the capacious umbrella of the poorhouse (Monkkonen 1993). Cities, with their highly varied and often innovative programs, finally lost most such activities in the fiscal crisis of the Great Depression. And federal highway planning — the basis of the transportation policy that ultimately undermined the railroads — was begun.

By the end of World War II, a new era of programs had emerged — new in the critical sense that local government's role had been diminished, with county, state, and federal governments now the big players. This era witnessed a significant departure from historical precedent, part of the larger transformation in the structure of the American state. For the first time a truly national state became visible, with a standing army, a shift in the tax base away from real property (yielding higher revenues from income taxes than from property taxes), and expenditure flows now moving from federal and state government to local governments. Federal aid to cities, unimaginable in any of the three previous eras, became permanent. Local programs now attracted federal, not local, funding.

In the same period, 1890–1935, urban reformers also began a political movement that would culminate in cities' making enormous strides toward legal independence and a more privileged constitutional standing in the states. Under the rubric of "home rule," local government began to escape the need to turn to the legislature for all small statutory changes. The phrase implies that cities gained more autonomy than they actually did, and it also implies a uniformity that home rule has never achieved. Dillon's "rule" still obtains (Schwartz 1973, 675–76). Yet the widely accepted concept of home rule did free cities from the kind of legislative actions represented in Appendix A for Illinois municipalities. And, even though in practice home rule is almost impossibly complex, the aims of its initial sponsors were achieved, somewhat ironically, even as the fiscal role of local government was slowly eclipsed by state and federal governments.

Even though historians have followed Thomas Cochran's advice to reject the "presidential synthesis" or periodization of the past (Cochran 1948), we still do our best thinking about politics and political thought and culture in the federal mode. Thus we have difficulty accepting the idea that in the nineteenth century, local governments acquired and spent far more money in total than state and federal governments. We forget that the income tax was a hastily dropped emergency measure during the Civil War, and that in the North, local governments often paid large sums to their Civil War volunteers. This mix, on which local governments leaned so heavily, was predicated on amicable relations between the various government levels.[3]

The federal government was, of course, perfectly willing to lend its modest resources to cities, even before the Civil War. Authorized by the Constitution and the Rivers and Harbors Act of 1826, for instance, the Army Corps of Engineers dredged harbors and rivers. Sometimes rather clever relationships between the Corps and cities developed. For instance, in the 1820s, Norfolk invested in the federal/state–built Dismal Swamp Canal. Further north, the Chesapeake and Ohio Canal, a federal-state venture, sold 25 percent of its stock to Alexandria, Georgetown, and Washington, D.C. A few years later, in Minnesota, out of a total government investment in railroads of $66 million, the federal government gave $60 million in land, but state and local governments contributed the most cash — $3 million each. And, in the 1850s, Richmond purchased a steam dredge, which it immediately leased to the U.S. Army (which thus paid for the city's dredge). Experienced army engineers supervised the whole river- and harbor-dredging project for the city (Elazar 1962).

Recent work on the American state — at both the state and the federal level (Gunn 1988; Skowronek 1982; Karl 1983; Keller 1977) — captures the U.S. nation-state's habitual speed at state building and deliberate shunting off to the private sector of operations likely to turn a profit. One might call this the minimal state, the stateless state, or the non-state state. The continuing model of the American state has been to assert fundamental power, lay down the ground rules, and then, if possible, bow out. Gunn contends that in the antebellum era, New York State used legislation to exit as quickly as possible from enterprises initiated and funded by government, turning them over to the private sector.[4] However, during this same era, local government expanded in capacity and fiscal power: the common-school movement, for instance, became a major local governmental investment.

Stephen Skowronek (1982) and Morton Keller (1977) assert that in the last part of the nineteenth century, the federal government deliberately avoided building regulatory bureaucracies. Yet it had in essence mandated such regulatory bodies as the Interstate Commerce Commission. Courts and parties steered government, Skowronek argues, and bureaucracies of experts stayed small and relatively limited. But during this era, states expanded their scope in charities, corrections, and economic regulation. And in the early twentieth century, the basic shape of the welfare state associated with the New Deal was worked out in detail at the level of state governments.

Barry Karl takes the story of American avoidance of state structures to the New Deal, where a genuine federal state-building effort unfolded while guided by this now well-established principle. Consequently, during this era, preexisting local bureaucracies often became the channels for federal funds. In sum, these historians of the three eras of American state building — the antebellum, post–Civil War through World War I, and New Deal–World War II eras — tell a similar tale, but about different levels in the federal system: state reluctance in the early years, federal reluctance later.

One can with some profit take these analyses and reconstruct from them a more positive picture of American state building. This view accepts the principle that by various means the American state prior to World War II had always avoided building its own bureaucracies, in part because these require tax revenues, a delicate issue in a nation built on a tax revolt. (The tariff, a way to collect revenue without direct taxes on voters, is the other route. To simplify, Democrats have historically opposed it; Whigs and, later, Republicans have not. Because it is a national form of taxation, it has been debated in national elections throughout the nineteenth and twentieth centuries.) To avoid taxation, American government has used lotteries and indirect subsidies, ranging from monopoly privileges (the classic toll roads and bridges) to general incorporation laws protecting investors through legal means, land subsidies for education and poor relief, aid to railroads, and tax-free land ownership for churches. Such subsidies accomplished something positive, and often associated with the more visible state building of Europe, by seemingly not doing anything at all.

Invisible state building also occurred in other ways. Robin Einhorn has detailed one category of hidden activity. Prior to 1860, sidewalk and street construction in Chicago never appeared in the city budget as an expenditure because of a system that allowed direct assessment and payment to contractors by property owners. The local, state, and federal financial support of railroads (through loans or land gifts) continued the tradition of no governmental interference in railroad construction. Planning and management were left to the railroad corporations, with governments simply providing the financial packages. Similarly, in cities, water companies, gas companies, and street-railway companies gained indirect subsidies via monopolies granted them by city councils (Jacobsen 1989). In addition, cities granted street railways lucrative speculative privileges in the suburban lands to which they ran their lines, so that the railroads captured the increased value of land as profit. English cities forbade this practice, which is why they had to subsidize railways directly (Ward 1964). American state action created minimal state bureaucracies: the state inhered essentially in rules and laws.

The places in which state building occurred were as diffuse as the state-made paper foundations for private enterprise were intangible. When state governments backed out of infrastructural development in the antebellum era, they simultaneously turned the promotional tasks over to local governments, townships, cities, and counties. When the federal government dealt uneasily with regulatory matters in the late nineteenth century, state governments took vigorous action (some of which met with Supreme Court resistance, as, for instance, in the case of railroad rate regulation). And when state and local welfare systems ran out of resources during the Great Depression, the federal government very visibly moved in.

Whether American state building occurred on the local, state, or

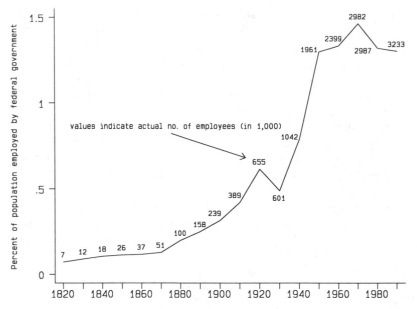

Figure 14. Growth in number of federal employees, as percentage of total population and in absolute numbers, 1820–1980. Source: *Historical Statistics of the United States, Colonial Times to 1970, Bicentennial Edition* (Washington, D.C.: USGPO, 1975).

federal level, it strove to avoid creating a permanent bureaucracy or even visible organization. Significant activities often occurred on a temporary basis: courts, for instance, met for a period, then the justices dispersed. Only after the Civil War and World War II did permanent federal bureaucracies take dramatic leaps, the percentage of the U.S. population employed by them in each time period climbing sharply (see Figure 14).

There are two highly significant contradictions to this overview of the American state, yet even these help explain the system. In two fundamental state activities this deliberate impermanence did not prevail: education and institutions dealing with the "dependent, defective, and delinquent classes," as so termed by Frederick Wines in the 1880 census. Even in the case of schooling, impermanence, or seasonality, characterized bureaucracies, with long vacations and highly variable student attendance. But school buildings became an early part of the built environment and a visible part of the American state. Similarly, persons who had to be cared for or locked up required permanent buildings and organizations. As opposed to, say, railroad management, their care could not easily be arranged through public subsidy of private enterprise. The one exception here is the convict lease system, which allowed southern state penitentiaries to provide what was virtually slave labor to labor-intensive agricultural factories, and county jails to provide the gang labor for road maintenance (Carleton 1971).

Not only did the poor and criminal gain permanent organizational establishments, but because some of their support or maintenance could not be handled with hidden subsidies, governmental budgets from very early on had to reflect these activities as direct cash expenditures. These all show up prominently in local budgets as high-spending categories. States copied one another in these provisions: in 1795, the laws of the Northwest Territory took their poor relief law directly from the Pennsylvania code, including the rate at which property was to be taxed (Pease 1925, 216–17). There were, of course, indirect subsidies to these institutions as well, most notably land set aside by state legislatures or constitutions, and under northwest territorial laws in Ohio, Illinois, Michigan, Minnesota, and Wisconsin (and later Mississippi and Alabama),[5] for poor farms and jails, or municipal lands donated for similar purposes (Pease 1925). Such buildings were prominent features of the nineteenth-century landscape, impressing people with one aspect of the local state: its intervention in the lives of children, the poor, and the delinquent.[6] The characteristically invisible American state became very visible and geographically fixed in these cases.

Current Crises in the Long View

Certain aspects of urban fiscal history have been well enough established to alter or emphasize some of the truisms about the urban fiscal crisis that seems to have begun in the early 1970s. The four main points to be emphasized here are (1) that the post–World War II era has been unusually stable and free of defaults; (2) that only the massive defaults of the 1930s demonstrate a nonrandom deviation from the historical series of defaults; (3) that most defaults have been "caused" in their deeper, as well as more immediate, sense by conscious political decisions; and (4) that the most important change since the Depression has been in the disassociation of residential property owners from the specifics of local finance.

The consequence of the latter development is that urban finance is now an arrangement worked out between financiers and multiple layers of government, with city dwellers, the formerly important third party, no longer included as directly interested participants. Recent experience in various state-level tax-limitation movements reinforces this point: taxpayers have complaints, many very specific, and some purely self-interested, and want changes in government (Sears and Citrin 1982). They can only make effective voting coalitions with meat-axe proposals, the most famous being California's Proposition 13, which affected local government dramatically, yet was impelled more by discontent with the *federal* government (Citrin and Levy 1981, 13).

Figure 15 and its inset, an amplification of the bottom, help illustrate the impact of the Depression on the shape of the postwar local revenue structure. The graph plots the date of each data point, so that timing may be examined. Several points should be emphasized. First, it is clear that the prewar period differed dramatically from the postwar period, in particular the period after the 1950s. The decades after World War II have been characterized by rising property tax revenues and rising expenditures on debt. Second, the two decades prior to 1950 saw relatively little variation in the revenues from property taxes compared to the wild variation in the proportion of budgets going to interest payments. This accounts for the appearance of the pedestal base at the bottom of Figure 15, the dramatic variation (horizontally) in interest expenditures for the two decades 1929–49, with almost no change in revenues (the vertical axis). Third, one major aspect of the general default crisis of the 1930s was the very high proportion of expenses going to pay interest on debt—as high as 8 percent of expenditures. Fourth, revenues from property taxes plunged to new lows during the Depression and stayed there until the postwar era.

Finally, one can see in the hook shape of the Figure 15 inset the

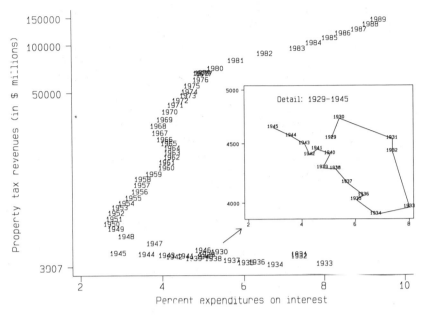

Figure 15. Total U.S. property tax revenues and percentage of expenditures for debt service, 1929–89. Sources: Calculated from *1977 Census of Governments,* vol. 6: *Topical Studies,* no. 4: *Historical Statistics on Governmental Finances and Employment* (Washington, D.C.: USGPO, 1978), supplemented with annual data from *National Income and Product Accounts of the United States* (Washington, D.C.: U.S. Dept. of Commerce, Bureau of Economic Analysis, USGPO, annual).

chronology of the Depression's impact on cities: revenues drop sharply from 1930 to 1934; not until 1933 do cities trim back from their debt-interest obligations; after 1933 they cut back on interest payments and begin to recover their tax revenues.

While Figure 15 shows the overall growth of property tax revenue, it fails to suggest the diminishing role played by these local taxes. Between 1902 and 1989, local taxes fell from 76 percent to only 18 percent of total local revenue, state and federal transfers contributing the remainder. In the context of historically high home ownership, and thus of property owners' concern about and control of city budgets, the diminishing role of property tax revenues indexes a more general distancing of homeowners from the local fiscal process.

The impact of federal transfers to local governments was amplified by the declining contribution of property taxes to city revenues. In the late 1920s and early 1930s, property taxes contributed most of state and local government receipts — around 60 percent. During the latter part of the Depression, this figure had dropped to a stable 45 percent. With the onset of World War II, a steady decrease began, which did not bottom out until 1980, when the proportion reached just under 18 percent (see Figure 4). Consequently, in the past fifty years the historic relationship of taxpayers to local government has been dramatically reversed. Had property tax contributions stayed high, the power of federal aid would have been considerably diluted. Federal aid to cities has acquired its significance because of the removal of voters from close ties of self-interest to fiscal policy, rather than by reason of federal policy alone.

Finally, the proportions of city expenditures going to meet interest payments are usually taken as an indicator of a city's general fiscal health. Again, the general picture for the 1970s is not nearly as grim as it was during the Depression. For instance, in the 1970s, 5 percent of all local government expenditures went for debt interest, in contrast to 8 percent in the mid 1930s (Figure 15). It is only in the more recent data for the 1980s that interest payments suggest a serious imbalance in post-Depression urban finance.

This imbalance has, in turn, created a new crisis, one with three dimensions: in services, in racial justice, and, of course, in finance. If nothing else, local urban government has legitimized itself, not as a governing body, but as a provider of services maintaining physical and social infrastructures, which in turn constitute the stage for social and economic action. Failure to provide any of these now-customary services undermines local government's legitimacy. For example, citizens now feel that they can demand freedom from crime, so the prevalence of crime and disorder threatens the very basis of local government. This expectation represents a fundamental shift toward greater government responsibility, bringing with it a deep problem: government does not really know how to control crime. Ironically then, U.S. city governments have acquired a major social engineering function that they may not be capable of providing. Social problems have become urban problems, and urban problems are the unique province of local government.

A crisis in racial justice follows from that in services. Those who have few choices in their residential areas and must live in central cities are disproportionately the victims of crimes. Recent immigrants, minority groups, the elderly, and the poor cannot escape to safer suburbs or different cities. Through no fault of their own, they cannot lead safe and predictable lives. The very dangers that make cities unattractive as residential centers multiply inward toward particular populations. The indirect costs of crime, then, are differentially borne by blacks, Latinos, and poor whites, while the direct costs of crime control amplify the city's fiscal stress and provide both a monetary and personal reason to escape. Although a disproportionate number of central city residents are violent offenders, others likewise suffer disproportionately. This unfair distribution of violent crime will not disappear even when the overall level of crime subsides, although its visibility may lessen.

The fundamental trajectory of U.S. urban history dates roughly from the second or third decade of the nineteenth century. During the Republic's first century, small but real crises were common occurrences. The more widespread, longer-lasting Depression of the 1930s was of a far different magnitude and embodied a difference of kind and of scale.

For crucial analytic reasons, the fifteen years following World War II should concern us more, in that they were the truly atypical years of prosperity for U.S. cities (if one grants that a century and a half is long enough to justify such an observation). The post–World War II era saw demographic and economic growth that was unprecedented in its magnitude, its smoothness, and its ability to exploit existing organizational structures without the buccaneering entrepreneurialism of the nineteenth century. The mid 1970s jolted U.S. cities with a hint of their traditional instability and proneness to crisis. The historical myopia of urban observers permitted them to see no further back in time than about 1956 and the Federal Highway

Act. Thus the unusual period of postwar growth and stability made the relatively minor crises of the 1970s loom prophetically and disproportionately large to a prosperous and wealthy generation.

For recent observers to be shocked at the city's servile position relative to financial institutions, or its deliberate efforts to make its inhabitants more economically productive, is to be unaware of the essence of the modern city. The essential model of the modern American city, developed in the mid nineteenth century, is non-regulatory and promotes both demographic and economic growth. To "discover" that cities work aggressively in these directions is to be either incredibly naive or historically ignorant. This conception of the ideal modern city is, in fact, new to the world. Its form was hammered out by experimentation and experience in the nineteenth century. It is not traditional. It has abandoned the tight control over social and economic affairs of its medieval predecessors. It has also abandoned its predecessors' strict hierarchies of inherited privilege and power. The modern U.S. city is already radically altered from the eighteenth century. And, as Michel Foucault might say, we have become a part of its discourse.

Urban Crises and History

While its conclusions vary, a constant theme has emerged from the past two decades of historical research on urban problems.[7] Irrespective of whether the subject is poverty, disease, social control, politics, or corruption, the findings run contrary to current wisdom on the state of the city. Crime rates have always been worse in the U.S. than in Europe; political corruption was greater in the U.S. past; class and ethnic conflict uglier; neighborhood instability greater; policymaking less consistent.

Thus, although the historian can share the amazement of others when examining the enormous growth in government expenditures since the 1960s, the fiscal and social straits of cities in the 1990s seem trivial when compared to local crises during the depressions of the 1930s, 1890s, and 1870s. Like old-timers recounting ever-worse blizzards, urban historians want to say, "Why, you should'a seen the soup lines in '93!" or, "Take a look at city reports from the depression, 'cause they won't last long — the city couldn't buy anything but newsprint for its published reports!" This backward look throws cold water on most speculation about the fiscal problems of cities in the post–World War II epoch, for it supports Richard Wade's claim that essentially things have never been so good for U.S. cities (Wade 1979).

Because historians so often draw their concerns from the present does not mean that they necessarily adduce evidence from the past to address present-day problems. Often, having found that "it" was "worse" in the "good old days," they also find "it" to have been so different as to preclude direct relevance to the present. Notwithstanding their hard-gained (and often counterintuitive) knowledge of the past, most urban historians make no claim to possess any special expertise on today's urban world to contribute. This is a pity, for the historian's view can provide important leverage in tackling current policy problems. History may not show the way to go, but it does indicate where others have been before us, and in so doing offers a healthy corrective to our excesses.

One of the arguments of this book is that previous crises were so large relative to current fiscal difficulties that calling today's urban financial problems "crises" is analytically incorrect. This does not mean that American local governments have no current fiscal problems. Obviously, they do. But it does mean that similar difficulties, often of much greater magnitude, have been faced before. Such problems are not unique to our era, and we should face them knowing what our predecessors did. We should know, too, that these problems are unlikely to be quickly resolved, and that the beneficiaries of our efforts may be a full generation away. This is a difficult proposition to accept, but absent the long view, we may end up sacrificing some of our predecessors' hard-won achievements.

We have forgotten some of the gains achieved in the era when the service apparatus of the modern city was still being formed. American cities no longer experience public health disasters like the Memphis yellow fever epidemic. The building of the modern service-oriented local government has been difficult and slow — and it will in all likelihood continue to be so. To define all current problems as crises diminishes what has been accomplished, and wrongly calls into question the modest machinery we have created.

Set in any reasonable time frame, the urban financial "crisis" that is seen as beginning in the mid 1970s is to a large extent an imaginary event, demarcated by very limited historical research and analysis, especially in the field of urban fiscal history. With only a handful of exceptions, the best literature on this so-called crisis has been written by nonhistorians, chiefly social scientists and journalists (Schefter 1977; Hoffman 1983; Fuchs 1992). Urban history has mainly been social history, and almost never city history. Those interested in urban political or economic crises have often gained some attention in the larger social science community, but social scientists are for the most part still woefully ahistorical, at least in the United States. This is, no doubt, one of the reasons why so few of those labeled urban historians have been asked to comment on a subject that has become its own scholarly subindustry in other social sciences.

The historian can make other important contributions to understanding the urban crisis aside from providing an empirical historical context. Many theoretical problems implicit in the study of the crisis also inform the historical study of urban institutions. These problems stand out more boldly when put in historical perspective, when it becomes evident that the reading of the past has all too often been used to bolster and justify theoretical positions rather than to develop critical insights.

Functionalists, too, often cast the city as a marvelous machine, functioning more smoothly than observers may at first comprehend: corrupt political bosses, in this view, were actually the unwitting handmaidens to a charmingly personal welfare system (Merton 1949). Social-control theorists, on the other hand, see deep crises, basic contradictions, and repression at every turn of events (Piven and Cloward 1971, 1977). The functionalists have the city cast as a passive responder, dealing with problems on an ad hoc and individual basis. The social-control theorists also see the city as a maintainer of the status quo, but doing so repressively, managing an inherently unstable social structure and crisis-prone economic system.

These two conflicting and fashionable models of the relationship of cities to poor people are important because each informs a separate analytic perspective on the larger urban crisis. Frances Piven and Richard Cloward (1977) saw New York's crisis of the 1970s in the social-control perspective, interpreting it as a near failure of the control mechanisms. The welfare system had failed in its main task of social control, the poor had begun to make political demands, and the crisis was a political subterfuge to rein in potentially revolutionary forces. The functionalists (Schultz et al. 1977) on the contrary saw the problem as a simple balance-sheet difficulty: too many poor people relative to the resources. Neither position makes descriptive claims of any great significance, the one claiming that the poor had become too powerful, the other that the city had become too poor. Historians are probably not guilty of the common accusation that they are atheoretical, but given the state of theory about urban crises and social control, their theory shyness certainly would be well justified.

Two historians did respond to New York City's crisis indirectly by writing about New York State's impending crises (McClelland and Magdovich 1981). The authors indicate that they had begun with the intention of producing a full-fledged econometric and historical analysis, but in the end had to satisfy themselves with organizational charts and an orderly list of data about the state's stupendously complex finances and indebtedness. Their book testifies convincingly to the difficult research problems that face anyone trying to alter the high proportion of bombast to data analysis in the literature on urban fiscal crisis. Untangling urban finance might drive the most avid researcher to the brink apparently reached by these writers, who ended up finding in Governor Nelson Rockefeller the causal mechanism that so eluded them in their search for decent data.

Even the briefest comparison of the crisis of the mid 1970s with the urban response to poverty during the Great Depression suggests the fatuity of both the functionalist and social-control analyses. As we have seen, the fourth-largest city in the country, Detroit, probably felt the swiftest, most severe impact during the Depression, when there were no federal programs for the poor. Across the United States, poverty became more widespread and desperate than ever before or, thus far, since. The significance of the urban impact of the Depression lies in its suddenness and directness: there were no multiple mediating agencies with varied sources of funding to cushion or diffuse the impact. One cannot help but be struck by the finality of the bank closures and subsequent bank holiday in 1931. Cities expended their cash on hand and then had no more monetary resources, period.

In contrast to the Depression's thousands of local government crises, the urban crisis of the 1970s had a much more widely diffused impact. Four actively involved governmental layers (city, county, state, and federal) and many more separately funded government agencies dealt directly with the crisis. The cushion of multiple sources of funds allowed administrators to ease short-run emergencies, to make transitions slowly, and in this way to make changes somewhat less dramatically visible.

Through programs like Aid to Families with Dependent Children and Social Security, the growth of the welfare state since the 1920s has mediated poverty on the individual level and diffused social responsibility. The orphanage lost clients with the advent of AFDC, while Social Security made it possible for many elderly people to stay in their own homes rather than go to the poorhouse. Although a theoretically alert examination of federal-city relations has yet to be done, there is no doubt that the welfare state has considerably eased the city's responsibility for the poor. This alone has probably had a greater impact on cities than any of the more sensational federal urban programs of the 1960s. Without Social Security and AFDC, the belt-tightening of fiscally troubled cities in the 1970s might have taken a different turn, and the poor might have suffered severely.

When Elliot Anthony, a Chicago delegate to Illinois's 1870 constitutional convention, reflected some twenty years later on the document that resulted, he maintained that it had stopped the practice of "the old days when public taxes and public funds could be diverted to private uses." The previous constitution had "put it in the power of the speculators of smaller municipalities to fasten mortgages on the taxpayers to help railroads, rolling mills, grist mills, coal mines, glass factories, woolen mills, and every variety of private enterprise" (Anthony 1891, 132). By limiting local debt, the 1870 constitution had kept "thieves and speculators" away from the "fat pastures" of public money (133). Yet it is now evident that Anthony must be interpreted cautiously, for he wanted a cap on state activities, not an end to them. Illinois voters approved limiting their own local governments' fiscal activities, even as they encouraged their local governments' pursuits of local development. These governments vigorously and constantly renegotiated actual local economic practice.

These same voters would therefore probably have agreed with Anthony's pronouncement that "the greatest engine of moral power known to human affairs is an organized, prosperous State" (125). Neither he nor the voters of Illinois intended to suppress completely the state promotion of economic enterprise. They made clear that they wanted a limited, but not insignificant, fiscal role for the state. The whole apparatus of the local state, including its fundamental law, the courts, and written constraints facilitated substantial pro-development activity within rhetorical and real confines. We must revise our understanding of this limited local state, for in actual practice it offered local governments much more room to maneuver than we have customarily understood. The contrast between then and now must be redrawn. Then, the power of the state was circumscribed, but it was positively conceptualized. Now, the state is less restricted, but it is seldom if ever conceptualized positively. For example, one can scarcely imagine our state apparatus being called the "greatest engine of moral power."

Bankers and voters, politicians and taxpayers, boosters and judges negotiated a politically complex public/private economic structure in the six decades between the Civil War and the Great Depression. All particulars and concrete instances originated on the local level. Abstract principle and actual opportunity often collided. Everyone involved could take seemingly contradictory stances, simultaneously voting for debt limits and more debt. Political contests over finance pitted Democrats and Republicans, factions, "rings," the wealthy, and the workers against one another. Sometimes the stakes were high and the losses big. Lenders could forfeit big sums, city dwellers could lose political control or even their city itself. The rules of the game evolved as it was played, each participant jockeying for advantage, while calling for moderation on the part of the others.

The regulatory response to municipal corporations strikingly paralleled the movement to regulate the private corporate world. Temporally, agitation for railroad rate regulation began at the state level in the mid 1870s. The regulation of cities also occurred at the state level, although the interstate commerce clause of the U.S. Constitution provided an opening for federal efforts to regulate corporate monopolies, resulting in the Sherman Act (1890) and the Clayton Act (1914). Unlike cities, industrial corporations turned to the federal government for control, in part because of the constitutional provisions in the interstate commerce clause and in part because they did business across many states. Major industries tried self-regulation through cartels designed to regulate prices, but these constantly fell apart as one member or another broke the agreements trying to gain advantage. Fearing destructive "cutthroat competition," many business leaders thus lent their ambivalent support to federal regulatory legislation, and a federal-corporate partnership was well established by World War I.

The analogy between private and public corporations goes only so far, however. Local governments had local monopolies but regional competition. Unlike business corporations, local governments did not have the option to form cartels or to merge with regional rivals. Taxpayers and voters were like combined railroad customers and owners. They did not want to pay high tax rates, yet they wanted their towns and cities to prosper. Thus until the very moment when regional regulation of all local governments leveled the playing field, they had to support local expenditures and aggressive borrowing. It is plausible that local governments wanted to limit their abilities to attract business so as to control competition with other cities and towns. This would explain why a place like Bishop, Illinois, could simultaneously borrow and vote to curtail its ability to do so. The only argument against this explanatory scenario is that the idea was nowhere voiced.

Additional changes in the nature of local government during the twentieth century have amplified this growth in local autonomy and power, in particular with the advent of city managers, commissions and at-large, nonpartisan elections. Created in the Progressive Era, these forms never gained a foothold in large cities, but they came to be the norm for smaller cities. This is significant in the context of the long-term increase in the number of small cities relative to large cities. As Figure 16, a reprise of Figure 1, exhibits,

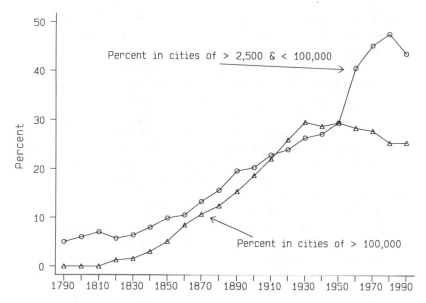

Figure 16. Percentage of total U.S. population in cities and towns with population greater than 2,500 and 100,000, 1790–1990. Sources: Calculated from *Historical Statistics of the United States, Colonial Times to 1970, Bicentennial Edition* (Washington, D.C.: USGPO, 1975) and *Statistical Abstract of the United States* (Washington, D.C.: USGPO, various dates).

the number of large cities (that is, those with over 100,000 inhabitants) began a long downturn in 1930, while the total number of cities has continued to increase. Forms of small-city government have thus become more important since the Depression. One intent of the reformers who introduced these forms was to put an end to urban corruption by severing local politicians from their neighborhood political bases and simultaneously putting city governments in the hands of experts. These ends were accomplished, but in concert with the fiscal transformation of the post-Depression era and the proliferation of small cities, they created a new and expanding local state, one virtually autonomous from voters and even from funding sources. This state is now represented by the large cadre of professionals who operate it, from the members of the City Managers' Association to the Association of City Engineers, the National Association of Elevator Safety Authorities, the Public Works Association, and numerous other organizations.

This new evolution of the local state has been both continuous and discontinuous with that worked out in detail by voters, judges, litigants, and city officials in the 1870s. It has been continuous in its local corporate status, its strategic use of incentives for private enterprise, and its competitive relationships. Conversely, Washington's new role, the supplanting of the railroads by federal interstate freeways, and the rise of state and federal income taxes as major sources of local government revenue sharply separates the postwar urban world from its predecessor.

In considering city affairs, it is essential to keep this uniquely American and federal dichotomy between politics and financing in mind. When federalism becomes an issue, as in Nixon's "New Federalism" program of the early 1970s, it really isn't very federal, so that further linguistic confusion occurs. In the case of the "New Federalism," the return to the states and local governments of their former status was to be accomplished through federal block grants. The intention was to reverse the undermining of local power on issues of racial discrimination under the Johnson administration. Block grants would be spent by state and local governments as they saw fit, not as the federal government did. But this kind of federalism resulted in federal expenditures on urban affairs rising even further than they had under Johnson. Ironically, then, the Nixon administration outspent both the Johnson and the Carter administrations for urban needs. The consequence was that the "New Federalism" actually increased the power of the federal government in local affairs even though it intended a redispersal of power.

The proportion of federal spending on state and local governments began to decrease with the Carter and then Reagan administrations, but the revenue capacity of the federal government has not been returned to local government. And as American colonial politicians told one another, the power to tax is the essential power for any government. The fact is that the Sixteenth Amendment (1913) gave the federal government its massive revenue capacity. This in turn made possible the New Deal response to the Depression and funded a huge standing army after World War II. Other new forms of federal revenue, such as the gasoline tax, funded an infrastructure designed for quick military mobilization, notably the federal highway system. These developments have permanently altered the city's status. Whereas public-private partnerships were once the most common way for cities and villages to accomplish large tasks, now local governments turn to the federal government as well. The local entrepreneurial spirit is still there, but the funding sources have changed.

The federal structure has provided alternative local financial units to accomplish the fiscal goals of cities. Typically, they depend on tax increment financing. In California, most notably, 1945 legislation enabled cities to create Community Redevelopment Agencies run by unelected administrators; often, but not always, their governing board is the city council, meeting as the CRA (Young 1991). What makes them special and powerful also makes them sound like something out of the nineteenth century (if not the Middle Ages): they may borrow money against expected increases in tax revenues. These revenues in essence belong to the CRA: they are its assets. The land controlled by the CRA must be designated as "blighted," but the definition of "blight" has proved in practice to be very flexible — from dilapidated buildings to high traffic counts. Consequently, some of the most valuable urban property in the United States is in CRA areas. Land use within the CRAs varies from malls to offices to industrial parks to hotels. Since 1983, California has required that a proportion of the CRAs' incomes go to low-income housing: the consequence — low-rise housing for seniors.

CRAs borrow money nominally and legally independently of city governments by issuing tax-increment revenue bonds. By working carefully with private developers and investors, and by controlling large land parcels, the CRAs are able to put together local economic packages that would have made the city officials of a century ago drool. Just as the federal structure of the United States has fostered thousands of independent and often very different local governments, it has also, through CRAs and their parallel agencies in other states, fostered a form of the local state that is purely concerned with private economic enterprise. Politically, today's suburban auto plaza shopping mall and hotel complex may well share deep similarities with a railroad repair shop in small-town nineteenth-century Illinois.

Was this a good way to run cities then? Is it a good way now? After two hundred years of constitutional government, the question may seem silly, but actually it underlies many critiques of urban affairs (Frug 1980). Some economic theorists argue that this is the best way (Tiebout 1956). Local governments compete against one another for the best revenue-generating activities, and this competition pushes the quality of city services up and their costs down. But some city services drive taxes up without directly encouraging business enterprises; Paul Peterson argues that some cities, by offering good welfare benefits, become "magnets" for the poor rather than magnets for business (Peterson 1981). If both Peterson and Charles Tiebout are correct, then the outcome might be an unstable and unequal mix of cities, the rich and the poor diverging sharply. And if they are right, we might expect that after another century of urbanism, the only equilibrating force between cities will be land values, which will soar in the places successfully offering the best tax/service packages. But will land values ultimately make places like Beverly Hills or Stamford simply too expensive, and the East St. Louises of the nation the destination of choice?

Or will more states move toward a kind of price control, where states regulate property taxes and local expenditures? This has begun to happen already with school expenditures in some states, including California. Beverly Hills, in fact, spends about the same per child as do much poorer cities.[8] If such price control affected other local services — police, fire, libraries, parks, and the like — one can imagine the competitive differences diminishing in power. In essence, that is what statewide debt limitation accomplished. There is little evidence that this has benefited East St. Louis, which is now even more desperately situated than it was in the nineteenth century. And there is no reasonable way to estimate how Illinois's cities and towns would have diverged without the debt limit. So we are left wondering if debt limits slowed economic growth, if they eased intercity competition, or if they did neither. Much of what I have found suggests the latter, that the limits functioned more as a safeguard, enabling cities to extricate themselves from bad deals.

In Browning's "Pied Piper of Hamelin," which has been mentioned several times in this book, we have an apt parable for comprehending the modern city. Browning juxtaposes the shortsighted greed of the mayor and medieval city corporation with future generations' well-being. Hamelin literally sells its future to solve its short-term problems. The specific moral of the poem, which is about keeping promises, links the body corporate to families, the children representing both the communal and the corporate future.

Current references to Browning's poem emphasize "paying the piper" rather than keeping promises. That the poem's narrative concerns a specific urban problem, one where the corporate city unintentionally and ignorantly sacrifices future generations to achieve an immediate solution, gives this still-popular "children's" poem enduring relevance. Is it not time for us to think back on the mayor and the children of Hamelin and better plan for our cities' futures?

Appendixes

APPENDIX A

Statutory Fiscal Limits of Illinois
Cities and Towns

In order to establish the record of special legislation in governing local finance, this list was compiled by a search of all the relevant Illinois laws prior to the new constitution of 1870. Most of the relevant material came in charters and charter amendments. The language of the legislation and the difficulty of an absolutely thorough search strategy make it clear that the information below should be understood as suggestive rather than as exhaustive or complete.

Take Metropolis as an example. Located in the very southern part of the state in Massac County, on the Ohio River, today it has just over 7,000 people. In 1870, its population numbered 2,490, more than double its 1,098 persons in 1860. Tax limits appeared in several sections of its 1845 incorporation act. Section 6 began, "The said trustees shall have power to levy and collect a tax, not exceeding one-half per cent., on all lots and improvements, and personal property, lying and being within the incorporated limits of said Metropolis city, according to valuation." The act continued to enumerate other sources of tax revenue, but without stating limits, for example enabling the town "to tax public shows and houses of public entertainment, stores and groceries." Section 10 dealt with "side walks" and in it appeared the limit "not to exceed one per cent" (*Laws of the State of Illinois, Passed by the Fourteenth General Assembly* [Springfield: Walters & Weber, 1845], 304–5). Six years later, in 1851, the acts of incorporation were amended, and section 1 of the amendment added the two-thirds of property owners approval requirement to the previous sidewalk tax (*Private Laws of the State of Illinois, Passed at the First Session of the Seventeenth General Assembly* [Springfield: Lanphier & Walker, 1851], 242). And, eight years later, a further incorporation amendment, in article VI, section 2, added language about borrowing: "The city council shall have power and authority to . . . borrow money and pledge the revenue of the city for the payment thereof: *Provided,* that no sum or sums of money shall be borrowed at a greater interest than ten per cent. per annum." This article gave further taxation powers, including, in section 16, an open provision for further taxation where "not fully provided in this charter" (*Laws of the State of Illinois, Passed by the Twenty-First General Assembly* [Springfield: Bailhache & Baker, 1859], 219–20).

What is reported in this appendix, then, are those portions of charters and other acts that set limits of some sort, and it is important to stress here that these limits do not establish the upper bounds of what taxes were authorized. Such might only be reconstructed by a careful reading and interpretation of all charters and amendments. The sources for the summaries below are the variously titled pre-1870 *Laws of the State of Illinois,* published in Springfield after 1840.

Alton (city). In 1837, taxes limited to 0.5% property tax, 0.25% school tax, and street labor of 3 days per year or $1 per day.

Alton (town). In 1837, borrowing limited to $300; (amended) tax limit added 0.25% property tax to fund schools.

Atlanta. In 1855, borrowing limited to $1,000, interest not to exceed 10% (referendum required if over $200).

Augusta. In 1859, taxes limited to 0.5% property tax; farmland subject only to school tax.

Aurora. In 1853, taxes limited to 0.5% property tax and 3 days per year street labor. In 1867, act legalizing CB&Q Railroad bonds; town could levy taxes, issue and/or borrow up to $50,000 at 10% interest, with $16,667 to be repaid each year.

Barry [Berry?] (formerly Worcester). In 1859, taxes limited to 0.5% property tax and 3 days per year or $1 per day street labor.

Belleville. In 1845, taxes limited to 0.5% property tax, 5 days per year or $1 per day street labor, and special sidewalk tax of 1.0%. In 1851, borrowed dollars not to exceed 10% interest. In 1853, bonds for street work authorized for $50,000 at 7% interest, an amount not to exceed one-half of property tax revenue. Also in 1853, additional borrowing limit of $50,000 imposed, at 10% interest, payable within 30 years and not to be sold below par. In 1854, property taxes limited to 0.20%, exclusively for funding public schoolhouses, with a required majority vote approval. In 1855, bonds for fire engine and market houses authorized, at 10% interest, redeemable within 10 years; taxes limited to a special school tax of 0.20%. Also in 1855, borrowing limited to a subscription of $50,000 in railroad bonds at 7% interest, redeemable within 20 years. In 1859, interest on city bonds not sold below par was limited to 10%, and a tax to pay interest of "5 mills/hundred" was authorized. Street labor limited to 3 days per year.

Belvedere. In 1852, borrowing limited to $2,000 at maximum 10% interest, with two-thirds voter approval; taxes limited to 1% property tax, special sidewalk tax by local ordinance, and street labor of 3 days per year.

Bentley. In 1869, taxes limited to 0.5% property tax and 3 days per year street labor.

Bloomington. In 1839, taxes limited to property tax not to exceed state law, special sidewalk tax with two-thirds approval required, and street labor of 3 days per year or $1 a day. In 1855, taxes included 0.20% school tax on property. In 1859, authorization of bonds issued for market at 6, 8, and 10% interest, redeemable in 1–15 years, all requiring a majority vote.

Brighton. In 1859, taxes limited to 0.5% property tax and 2–5 days per year street labor.

Brooklynn. In 1855, taxes limited to 0.5% property tax and 2–5 days per year street labor.

Cairo. [Records incomplete.] In 1859, interest rate on borrowing increased from 6 to 10%; taxes limited to special sidewalk tax requiring two-thirds voter approval.

Caledonia. In 1837, taxes limited to 1% property tax; could levy additional tax for schools.

Carlinville. In 1837, taxes limited to 1% property tax; special sidewalk tax of 1% upon two-thirds voter approval. In 1853, taxes limited to 0.5% property tax; street labor limited to 3 days per year or $1 per day.

Carmi. In 1840, taxes limited to 0.5% property tax; special sidewalk tax with two-thirds voter approval.

Centralia. In 1859, taxes limited to 0.25% on property. Raised after 3 years with two-thirds vote; special sidewalk tax with two-thirds petition; street labor of 3 days per year or $1 per day.

Chester (city). In 1855, taxes limited to 1% property tax; special sidewalk tax with two-thirds vote; street labor of 3 days per year or amount to be determined. In 1859, taxes limited; street labor replaced with 0.25% tax.

Chester (town). In 1837, taxes limited to increase in ad valorem tax on town lots, not to exceed 3%, with consent of two-thirds of voters. In 1839, taxes limited to 2% property tax but no tax greater than 0.5% without three-fourths vote; could levy additional school tax; borrowing limited to funds for public improvement, with two-thirds vote; special sidewalk tax with two-thirds petition. In 1843, incorporation act repealed. In 1845, legalized acts to pay off debts; taxes limited to a special 2% tax; tax limited to a 0.75% tax thereafter [further meaning unclear].

Chicago. In 1835, taxes limited to 0.5% property tax and sidewalk tax with two-thirds approval. In 1841, borrowing limited to Cook Co. borrowing $10,000 at 8% interest, not to exceed 20 years, funded at par. In 1845, tax limited to school tax of $1 million with other taxes limited to $2.5 million. In 1851, borrowing limited: city could borrow $100,000; taxes limited to 0.35% property tax, 0.20% school tax, 0.05% debt repayment, 2% tax for lake barrier and city hall; borrowing limited to borrowing for marketplace. In 1854, borrowing limited to $100,000 for waterworks and a tax on debt of $1 million. In 1863, borrowing limited to $12,000 for State St. bridge, at 7% interest; borrowing limited to bonds (general) not to exceed $100,000 at 7% interest; tax limited to 0.45% tax for general fund, 0.20% school tax, 0.20% police tax, 0.10% reform school tax, 0.20% street lighting tax, a tax for "sufficient" sewerage, a tax limited to one "sufficient" to pay interest on debt, a tax limited to 0.25% for public buildings, a tax limited to one "sufficient" to pay preceding years' debt, and a tax limited to 0.10% for a sinking fund. In 1863, street labor abolished; borrowing limited to waterworks bonds, $500,000 maximum at 7% interest, not to be sold below par without two-thirds vote of aldermen; borrowing limited to sewerage bonds, also $500,000 at 7% interest, not to be sold below par without two-thirds vote of aldermen, with a sinking fund not greater than 2% of amount of bonds.

Clinton. In 1855, taxes limited to 0.5% property tax and street labor of 3 days per year or $1 per day.

Collinsville. [Records incomplete.] Tax limited to 0.5% property tax.

Columbia. In 1855, taxes limited to 0.5% property tax; special sidewalk tax only with two-thirds voter approval.

Columbus. In 1855, taxes limited to 0.5% property tax and street labor of 3 days per year or $1 per day.

Creston. [Records incomplete.] In 1869, taxes limited to 2% property tax.

Dallas City. In 1859, taxes limited to 0.5% property tax; borrowing for schools limited to 7% interest, aggregate interest not to exceed one-half of revenue arising from property tax; sidewalk tax allowed by local ordinance; street labor limited to 5 days per year or $1 per day.

Danville. In 1839, taxes limited to 1% property tax; borrowing for schools only with two-thirds voter approval; sidewalk tax only with two-thirds approval. In 1855, taxes limited to 0.5% property tax; street labor limited to 3 days per year or $1 per day. In 1863, borrowing limited to bonds for bridge, $20,000 at 10% interest, payable in 1–2 years by a special tax for 2 years.

Decatur. In 1839, taxes limited to 1% property tax; tax limited to additional school tax with two-thirds voter approval; sidewalk tax only with two-thirds voter approval; street labor limited to 4 days per year or $1 per day. In 1854, taxes limited to 0.5% property tax. In 1855, borrowing limited at 10% interest rate, aggregate interest not to exceed one-half of property tax revenue; sidewalk tax limited by local ordinance; street labor limited to 3 days per year or $1.25 per day.

Desplaines. In 1869, borrowing limited to $5,000 at 10% interest as approved by a majority of voters; taxes limited to property tax limited by state law; street labor limited to 3 days per year or $1.50 per day.

Dixon. In 1853, taxes limited to 0.5% property tax; borrowing limited to money for public works ("on such terms shall seem best"); sidewalk tax only with two-thirds voter approval. In 1859, taxes limited to 0.25% property tax.

Edwardsville. In 1853, taxes limited to 0.5% property tax; street labor limited to 2–5 days per year; borrowing limited to bonds issued for plank roads: borrowing limited to $5,000 at 10% interest plus a 1% special tax to pay debt. In 1859, borrowing limited to railroad subscription: $30,000 at 10% interest as approved by a majority of voters; taxes limited to a "sufficient" tax for interest.

Elgin. In 1854, taxes limited to 0.5% property tax and a 0.25% school tax; borrowing limited to 10% interest, aggregate interest not to exceed one-half of property tax revenue as approved by two-thirds of the voters; sidewalk tax limited by local ordinance; street labor limited to 3 days per year or $1 per day. In 1855, taxes limited to 0.25% tax to fund roadwork plus a 0.5% school tax.

Eureka. In 1859, taxes limited to property tax by state law; street labor limited to 3 days per year.

Ewington. In 1855, taxes limited to 0.5% property tax.

Fairview. In 1859, taxes limited to 0.5% property tax; sidewalk tax limited by local ordinance; street labor limited to 3 days per year or $1 per day.

Freeport. In 1855, taxes limited to 0.5% property tax; borrowing limited to 10% interest, aggregate interest not greater than one-half of property tax revenue, as approved by a majority of voters; street labor limited to 3 days per year or $1 per day.

Fulton. In 1859, taxes limited to 0.5% property tax, street labor limited to 3 days per year or $1 per day; no money borrowed without majority vote.

Galena. In 1837, taxes limited to 0.5% property tax; sidewalk tax with two-thirds voter approval. In 1839, taxes limited to street labor of 3 days per year or $1 per day. In 1845, street labor repealed. In 1852, taxes limited to 1% property tax; tax limited to additional 1% tax for debt payment. In 1853, borrowing limited to issue of bonds to railroad, for $100,000 at 8% interest, with tax limited to a tax to pay interest.

Galesburg. In 1841, taxes limited to 1% property tax; borrowing limited; street labor limited to 1–3 days per year or $1 per day. In 1863, borrowing limited to funds needed for county building at 10% interest with taxes limited to a tax to pay interest.

Geneseo. In 1855, taxes limited to 0.5% property tax (1% with voter approval); street labor limited to 3 days per year or $1 per day.

Golconda. In 1845, taxes limited to 0.5% property tax and 1% sidewalk tax by two-thirds voter approval.

Grafton. In 1853, taxes limited to 1% property tax; street labor limited to 5 days per year; sidewalk tax limited to that approved by two-thirds vote.

Grayville. In 1839, taxes limited to 0.5% property tax. In 1851, tax limited to sidewalk tax by majority voter approval. In 1855, tax limited to street labor of 3 days per year or $1 per day.

Greenup. In 1855, taxes limited to 0.5% property tax; sidewalk tax only with majority voter approval.

Greenville. In 1855, taxes limited to 0.5% property tax; tax limited to street labor of 3–5 days per year.

Hamilton. In 1859, taxes limited to 0.5% property tax; borrowing limited to $10,000 at 10% interest.

Havana. In 1853, taxes limited to street labor of 2–4 days per year or $1 per day.

Hennepin. In 1839, taxes limited to 0.5% property tax. In 1852, taxes limited to street labor of 2 days per year or $0.75 per day.

Henry. In 1854, taxes limited to 0.5% property tax; borrowing limited to 8% interest with aggregate interest not greater than one-half of property tax revenue; street labor tax limited to 3 days per year or $1 per day. In 1859, tax limited to 0.5% tax for city and road purposes; borrowing limited to aggregate debt not greater than $300 without vote.

Highland. In 1863, taxes limited to 0.5% property tax.

Hillsboro. In 1855, taxes limited to 0.5% property tax and street labor limited to 2–3 days per year or $1 per day.

Hutsonville. In 1853, taxes limited to 0.5% property tax; borrowing limited to 10% interest with aggregate interest not greater than one-half of property tax revenue; street labor limited to 3 days per year or $1 per day; sidewalk tax limited by local ordinance.

Illinoistown. In 1859, taxes limited to 0.5% property tax; street labor tax limited to 2–5 days per year or $1 per day.

Jerseyville. In 1837, taxes limited to 0.5% property tax; sidewalk tax only with two-thirds voter approval; street labor limited to 3 days per year or $1 per day. In 1855, taxes limited to 1% property tax.

Joliet. In 1852, taxes limited to 1% property tax; borrowing limited to 10% interest with aggregate interest not greater than one-half of property tax revenue; street labor limited to 3 days per year or $1 per day. In 1853, taxes limited to 0.20% additional school tax.

Juliet (Joliet after 1845). In 1841, taxes limited to 0.25% property tax.

Kankakee. In 1839, taxes limited to 0.5% property tax; borrowing limited to $10,000 for bridges and other improvements; taxes limited to tax to repay debt not greater than interest on sum. In 1855, taxes limited to 1% property tax; street labor limited to 3 days per year or $1 per day.

Kansas. In 1859, taxes limited to 0.5% property tax and street labor of 3 days per year or $1.50 per day.

Kaskaskia. [Records incomplete.] In 1818, taxes limited to 2% property tax.

Knoxville. In 1845, taxes limited to 0.25% property tax; street labor limited as required; 1% sidewalk tax by two-thirds voter approval; borrowing limited to not more than total taxes for year. In 1853, tax limited to 0.5% property tax; borrowing limited to 8% interest with aggregate interest not greater than one-half of property tax revenue; sidewalk tax limited by local ordinance; street labor limited to 4 days per year or $0.75 per day. In 1853, special act passed to subscribe to railroad with borrowing limited to $15,000 at 8% interest, to be funded at par. Additional stock purchases required a vote.

La Harpe. In 1859, taxes limited to 0.5% property tax; sidewalk tax limited to that allowed by local ordinance; street labor limited to 3 days per year or $1 per day.

La Salle. In 1852, taxes limited to 0.5% property tax; borrowing limited to 10%, with aggregate interest not greater than one-half of property tax revenue; sidewalk tax limited by local ordinance; street labor limited to 3 days per year or $1 per day. In 1853, act passed to renew loan specified in 1853 charter [unavailable].

Lacon. In 1839, taxes limited to 1% property tax; additional school tax could be assessed; borrowing limited to money for public works with a majority vote; sidewalk tax required two-thirds voter approval. In 1853, borrowing limited to $20,000 at 10% interest, payable annually within 20 years, with a special tax for interest payment. In 1854, borrowing limited to that approved by majority vote; sidewalk tax required local ordinance; street labor limited to 4 days per year or $0.75 per day; borrowing limited to 10% interest, payable annually within 20 years, with a special 1% property tax to pay interest; farmland exempt, but subject to 1% property tax to pay interest on debts.

Lawrenceville. In 1835, tax limited to 0.5% property tax; sidewalk tax required two-thirds voter approval.

Liberty. [Records incomplete.] In 1839, property tax could be increased to 2.5% to fund public improvements; borrowing limited to 20-year bonds for securing riverbank and for street and alley improvement.

Limestone. [Records incomplete.] In 1863, taxes limited to 1% property tax for payment to Kankakee Bridge Co.

Litchfield. In 1859, taxes limited to 1% property tax; sidewalk tax allowed upon two-thirds voter approval; borrowing limited to not more than 5 years with no bonds greater than 2% of assessed property value.

Little Fort. [Records incomplete.] In 1852, special fire department tax allowed at 0.5% for first two years, 0.25% thereafter. Borrowing limited to payment of cemetery debt; sidewalk tax required owners to maintain at own expense.

Lockport. [Records incomplete.] In 1853, taxes limited to 0.5% property tax; street labor limited to 1–3 days per year or $1.25 per day (as a poll tax); borrowing not to surpass tax revenue without majority vote.

Macomb. [Records incomplete.] In 1841, taxes limited to 0.5% property tax; sidewalk tax allowed by two-thirds voter approval. In 1855, borrowing limited to no more than 8% interest, with aggregate interest not greater than one-half of property tax revenue. In 1859, no railroad subscriptions to be made without voter approval.

Manchester. [Records incomplete.] In 1843, taxes limited to street labor as provided by law.

Marion. In 1841, taxes limited to property tax not greater than that allowed by state law; sidewalk tax required two-thirds voter approval; taxing or borrowing for schoolhouse and support of common schools required two-thirds vote; street labor limited to 3 days per year or $1 per day.

Marshall. In 1853, taxes limited to 0.5% property tax; sidewalk tax only by majority approval. In 1855, borrowing limited to no more than 7% interest, aggregate interest not to be greater than one-half of property tax revenue; sidewalk tax to be approved by local ordinance; street labor limited to 3 days per year or $1 per day.

Mattoon. In 1854, taxes limited to 0.5% property tax; sidewalk tax allowed by local ordinance; street labor limited to 3 days per year or $1 per day.

McHenry. In 1855, taxes limited to 0.25% property tax. In 1859, an incomplete 1853 act repealed.

Mendota. In 1859, taxes limited to 1% property tax and street labor of 3 days per year.

Metropolis City. In 1845, taxes limited to 0.5% property tax; sidewalk tax required two-thirds voter approval at 1% maximum. In 1851, sidewalk tax required two-thirds approval. In 1859, borrowing limited to 10% interest or less, approved with a majority vote; sidewalk tax as by local ordinance, owners to construct at own expense.

Moline. In 1855, taxes limited to 0.5% property tax, sidewalk tax by local ordinance, and street labor limited to 3 days per year. In 1855, borrowing limited to $3,000 at 10% interest with two-thirds voter approval. In 1863, borrowing limited to $3,000 (i.e., 10% interest limit removed).

Monmouth. In 1852, taxes limited to 0.5% property tax; borrowing limited to 7% interest, aggregate interest not greater than one-half of property tax revenue; street labor limited to 3 days per year or $0.75 per day.

Morris. In 1853, taxes limited to 0.75% property tax.

Mound City. [Records incomplete.] In 1859, taxes limited to 0.5% property tax plus sidewalk tax by local ordinance.

Mt. Carmel. In 1825, taxes limited to 1.5% property tax. In 1835, taxes limited to 1% property tax. In 1851, taxes limited to sidewalk tax by one-half voter approval; borrowing limited to subscription to AM&A Railroad, $100,000 at 10% interest, and to Mt. Carmel Mfg. Co., $100,000 at 10% interest, both requiring majority vote. In 1859, borrowing limited to subscription to Ohio R&W Railroad of $50,000 at 10% interest; this amended the 1% property tax limit.

Mt. Pulaski. In 1854, taxes limited to 0.5% property tax; sidewalk tax allowed by two-thirds voter approval; street labor limited to 2–5 days per year.

Nashville. In 1853, taxes limited to 1% property tax; special school tax by majority vote; sidewalk tax by two-thirds voter approval.

Nauvoo. In 1841, taxes limited to 0.5% property tax; street labor limited to 3 days per year or $1 per day. In 1845, borrowing limited to money for railroad or plank road: a limit of $50,000 at 10% interest for not longer than 20 years.

New Boston. In 1859, taxes limited to 0.5% property tax; special tax authorized should city subscribe to a railroad; borrowing limited to less than 10% interest, aggregate interest not greater than one-half of property tax revenue; sidewalk tax as approved by local ordinance; street labor limited to 4 days per year or $1 per day.

New Haven. In 1839, taxes limited to 0.5% property tax.

Oquawka. [Records incomplete.] In 1852, borrowing authorized town to subscribe to plank road or ferry company, limited to ferry for $25,000, plank road for $10,000, at 8% interest. City had to create a special tax to pay debt, requiring a majority vote.

Ottawa. In 1837, taxes limited to 1% property tax; sidewalk tax required two-thirds voter approval. In 1853, taxes limited to 0.5% property tax; borrowing limited to 10% interest with a majority vote; could subscribe to bridge company with a majority vote; sidewalk tax at owners' expense.

Palestine. In 1855, taxes limited to 0.5% property tax; sidewalk tax required two-thirds voter approval.

Paris. In 1853, taxes limited to 0.5% property tax; sidewalk tax by local ordinance; street labor limited to 3 days per year or $1 per day. In 1859, 1853 act repealed.

Pekin. In 1839, taxes limited to 1% property tax; sidewalk tax required two-thirds voter approval; street labor limited to 3 days per year or $1 per day; town could not tax merchants, auctioneers, tavern-keepers, or ferries until county relinquished such revenue. In 1853, borrowing limited to money for plank road or embankment: $100,000, with special tax to pay interest. In 1854[?], town could contract with ferry or railroad to cross river, but could not construct bridge across river without act of legislature.

Peoria. In 1837, taxes limited to 0.5% property tax; sidewalk tax required two-thirds voter approval; could not tax merchants, etc., until county relinquished such revenue; borrowing limited to money for bridge: $50,000 at 7% interest, not to exceed 15 years or to be sold under par. In 1844, property tax limited to 0.75%; borrowing limited to 6% interest, aggregate interest not greater than one-half of property tax revenue; street labor limited to 3 days per year or $1 per day; borrowing allowed for subscription in Peoria and Oquawka Railroad. In 1845, borrowing limited to money for waterworks at 6% interest with a majority vote and a special debt/interest tax. In 1853, borrowing limited to subscriptions in any railroad stock: $300,000 at 10% interest, bonds not to be sold under par, majority vote required. In 1863, borrowing allowed for bonds to replace funds taken from railroad fund and used to pay school bonds: limited to $10,000 at 7–8% interest, with a 0.1% property tax to pay interest.

Peru. In 1845, taxes limited to 0.5% property tax; sidewalk tax required two-thirds voter approval. In 1851, borrowing limited to 8% interest, aggregate interest not greater than one-half of property tax revenue; sidewalk tax required local ordinance; street labor limited to 3 days per year or $1 per day; borrowing allowed for subscription to railroad stock: $25,000 to RI&L Railroad with borrowing limited to $50,000; to any other railroad with Peru terminus at no more than 6% interest with a majority vote. In 1853, taxes allowed for additional levy to pay railroad bonds and a special tax for schools (to be kept separate from general fund) with an aggregate interest limitation. Not applicable to public improvement bonds approved by voters; also, a tax limited to toll to pay for turnpike.

Petersburg. In 1841, taxes limited to 0.5% property tax; street labor limited to 2–4 days per year or $1 per day.

Pittsfield. [Records incomplete.] In 1837, town could increase ad valorem tax on town lots to 3% with three-fourths consent of lot owners.

Polo. In 1859, taxes limited to 0.10% property tax; sidewalk tax at owners' expense; street labor limited to 3 days per year or as a poll tax at $1.25 per day.

Princeton. [Records incomplete.] In 1854, taxes limited to 1% property tax for plank road; tax required majority vote.

Prophetstown. In 1859, taxes limited to 0.5% property tax; street labor limited to 3 days per year or $1 per day; sidewalk tax by local ordinance.

Quincy. In 1839, taxes limited to 1% property tax; sidewalk tax with majority consent; street labor limited to 3 days per year or $1 per day. In 1840, taxes limited to 0.5% property tax; borrowing limited to 6% interest, aggregate interest not greater than one-half of property tax revenue. In 1841, tax limited to school tax of one-eighth of 1%. In 1851, taxes limited to a special tax to pay interest on railroad bonds. In 1853, borrowing limited to subscription to Northern Cross Railroad with borrowing limited to $100,000 at par with majority vote. In 1855, tax approved for $2 annual fee for all males over eighteen, replacing street labor tax. In 1859, taxes limited to gaslight tax of 0.28% (on lighted area), 0.25% school tax; any other tax greater than 0.18% required majority vote.

Rock Island. In 1841, taxes limited to 0.5% property tax and sidewalk tax requiring two-thirds voter approval. In 1852, borrowing limited to subscription to Chicago & Rock Island Railroad, borrowing limited to $50,000 at 10% with a tax to pay interest.

Rockford. In 1853, borrowing limited to money for public bridges; limited to $15,000 at 10% interest, repayment not to exceed 20 years, with a special tax to pay interest. In 1854, taxes limited to 0.5% property tax; borrowing limited to not more than 12% interest, aggregate interest not greater than one-half of property tax revenue; street labor limited to 3 days per year or $0.75 per day; further tax limited to additional school tax.

Rockton. [Records incomplete.] In 1853, borrowing limited to money for public buildings. Borrowing limited to $10,000 at 10%, not to exceed 20 years, with majority vote at town meeting.

Rushville. [Records incomplete.] In 1839, taxes limited to 0.5% property tax; sidewalk tax required two-thirds voter approval; street labor limited to 2–5 days per year.

Sandoval. In 1859, taxes limited to 0.5% property tax; sidewalk tax for which owners paid one-half of the expense. Street labor limited to 4 days per year or $1 per day.

Shawneetown. [Records incomplete.] In 1835, taxes limited to "other taxes" of 0.25%.

Shelbyville. In 1839, taxes limited to 1% property tax; sidewalk tax required two-thirds voter approval. In 1863, taxes limited to 0.5% property tax; sidewalk tax required ordinance and limited to not greater than cost; street labor limited to 2 days per year.

Sparta. In 1859, taxes limited to 0.5% property tax; sidewalk tax required local ordinance; borrowing limited to 10% interest, aggregate interest not greater than one-half of property tax revenue; street labor limited to 4 days per year or $1 per day, with only one-fourth of labor tax to be used on roads outside town limits.

Springfield. In 1837, taxes limited to 4% property tax on extended boundary areas; sidewalk tax required two-thirds voter approval; borrowing limited to $100,000. In 1840, taxes limited to 0.5% property tax; sidewalk tax required local ordinance; street labor limited to 3 days per year or $1 per day; borrowing limited to 10% interest, aggregate interest not greater than one-half of property tax revenue. In 1843, taxes limited to 2% tax to pay bonds for State Bank of Illinois. In 1845, this act repealed and borrowing limited to no more than could be repaid with annual tax revenues. In 1854, borrowing limited to interest not greater than allowed by law and aggregate interest not greater than one-half of property tax revenue, bonds not to be sold under par; sidewalk tax required local ordinance and at owners' expense; tax limited to 0.5% property tax plus special taxes: 0.5% school tax, 0.5% debt tax, 0.5% public improvements tax, 0.5% drains and sewer tax; street labor limited to 3 days per year or $2 for all or $3 if past 10 days per year [meaning unclear].

St. Charles. In 1853, taxes limited to 1% property tax, street labor of 3 days per year. Borrowing included subscription to St. Charles Railroad at 10% interest, to be sold at par with the time of payment fixed so that payments on debt and interest not greater than $3,000 per year, all requiring a majority vote.

Staunton. In 1859, taxes limited to 0.5% property tax; street labor limited to 2–5 days per year; sidewalk tax: owners pay one-half.

Sterling. [Records incomplete.] In 1859, borrowing limited to 10% interest, aggregate interest not greater than one-half of property tax revenue.

Teutopolis. In 1845, taxes limited to 0.5% property tax, 2–5 days per year street labor, and sidewalk tax requiring two-thirds voter approval.

Thebes. In 1852, taxes limited to 0.35% property tax, sidewalk tax after approval by two-thirds voter majority, with owners to bear three-fourths of expense.

Toulon. In 1859, taxes limited to 0.5% property tax and street labor of 3 days per year.

Tremont. In 1841, taxes limited to 0.25% property tax; borrowing limited to money for public works ($1,000 total).

Triskilwa (formerly Indiantown). In 1855, taxes limited to a sidewalk tax not greater than one-half of the cost and street labor of 3 days per year.

Upper Alton. In 1837, taxes limited to 1% property tax, additional school tax by majority vote, and sidewalk tax requiring two-thirds voter approval.

Urbana. In 1855, taxes limited to 1% property tax; borrowing limited to 10% interest, aggregate interest not greater than one-half of property tax revenue. Street labor limited to 3 days per year or $1 per day.

Vienna. In 1841, taxes limited to 0.5% property tax and sidewalk tax not greater than 1%, by two-thirds vote. In 1859, taxes limited to property tax not greater "than by law"; sidewalk tax required local ordinance; street labor of 5 days per year or $1 per day.

Warren (JoDavies Co). In 1859, taxes limited to 0.5% special property (real and personal) tax for paying off debt and making improvements, requiring a majority vote. Street labor limited to 2 days per year plus an additional day for every $500 in assessed property, or $1 per day.

Warsaw. In 1837, taxes limited to land in lots. In 1839, taxes limited to 1% property tax, sidewalk tax requiring two-thirds voter approval, and street labor of 3 days per year or $1.25 per day. In 1853, tax limit changed to 0.5% property tax, with borrowing limited to 6% interest, aggregate interest not greater than one-half of property tax revenue. Borrowing for railroad and plank road limited to $100,000 at 10% interest, bonds not to be sold under par (formerly had excepted railroad and plank road). At some later unclear date, the railroad was to receive city bonds at par in lieu of cash. In 1855, borrowing limited to bonds for school building, $10,000 at 10% interest, with a special 1% tax for repayment. In 1859, borrowing limited to interest rate not greater than one-half of property tax revenue; taxes limited to 0.10% for sewers and drains (whenever majority petitioned for same); taxes for sidewalk limited by local ordinance at owners' expense. The city council could incur no debt without simultaneously creating a tax sufficient for repayment; a portion of the general fund had to be set aside annually to pay interest on the debt; an additional school tax was limited to one-eighth of 1%. In 1863, 1859 charter repealed, making Warsaw a township.

Waterloo. In 1849, taxes limited to 0.5% property tax; sidewalk tax required two-thirds voter approval. In 1859, taxes limited to 0.75% property tax.

Waukegan (formerly Little Fort). In 1853, taxes limited to 0.5% property tax, sidewalk tax requiring local ordinance, at not greater than cost, and street labor of 3 days per year or $1 a day. Borrowing limited to 10% interest with a majority vote. In 1855, borrowing limited to bridges, $20,000 at 12% interest, with 20-year limit; tax limited to special tax not greater than 0.5% for payment of debt and to a special tax to maintain bridges. In 1859, taxes limited to 0.80% property tax with street labor commuted at $0.75 per day (defaults at $1.25 per day) and a limited school tax of 0.4%. In 1859, borrowing limit amended: no money could be borrowed, nor could the town subscribe to or lend money to benefit a private corporation.

West Belleville. [Records incomplete.] In 1859, borrowing limited to 10% interest.

Wilmington (formerly Winchester; Will County). [Records incomplete.] In 1852, taxes limited to annual levy for a bridge: $1,500 for each year.

Winchester (Scott County). In 1846, taxes limited to 0.5% property tax, street labor of 2–5 days per year, and sidewalk tax requiring two-thirds voter approval.

Woodstock (formerly McHenry). In 1852, taxes limited to 0.75% property tax; sidewalk tax required two-thirds voter approval. Owners to pay three-fourths of expense.

Local Debt in the States, 1880

The Bureau of the Census gathered some fiscal data that allow a highly aggregated overview of the impact of the number of cities and the impact of state debt limits on local debt. These data are aggregated by state and so may wash out within state variations. The three estimates in Tables B1–3 show that the state's age increased debt, the number of cities in the state (per capitized) decreased debt, and that limits showed no impact on debt. The number of cities (over 7,500 persons) per the total population of the state has been used to capture the borrowing ability of multiple units of government (see Table B1).

A regression similar to the one in Table B1 can be estimated as an alternative test (see Table B2). This equation uses the per capita local debt in 1880 as the dependent variable and a similar value for 1870 (prior to the debt limits in all states) as an independent variable that cumulates the impact of all prior actions affecting debt, such as region, age of state, and unknown ecological factors. To this is added a single additional indepen- dent variable, namely whether or not the state had debt limitation. Mary- land and Maine have been excluded as outliers, although the equation estimates are similar with them included. The two per capita debt figures may differ slightly because that for 1870 is based on all cities with a popula- tion of more than 4,000, as opposed to 7,500. The estimate results confirm the test above. Limitation had no effect on per capita local debt.

Finally, a stepwise regression can be estimated allowing the limitation variable to drop out and considering several 1870 variables (see Table B3). Here, once again, the number of cities per capita in 1870 has a significant and negative effect on local debt a decade later.

TABLE B1

Impact of Age, Region, and Cities on Local Debt, 1880

Variable	Coefficient	(SEE)	F	Sig.
Age (years since 1790)	.43	(.077)	31.69	.0000
Region[a]	−15.52	(4.83)	10.34	.0029
Cities[b] per 100,000	−3.21	(.992)	10.44	.0028

SOURCES: For 1880 debt, U.S. Census Office 1884. For 1870 debt, U.S. Census Office 1872a. Population data calculated from U.S. Bureau of the Census 1883.

NOTE: Dependent variable: net debt per capita for all cities in state with populations of over 7,500. Adj. R-square = .665. Constant = 91.786.

[a]States were scored one for South, two for North. A dummy variable for limit and one for cities per capita were not included in a stepwise regression, where their probabilities would have been .896 and .510 respectively. All but three debt ceilings were established prior to 1877. States with ceilings (as percentage of taxable real estate) or tax limits, with the dates of their limits, included: Maine, 5% ceiling (1877); Pennsylvania, 7% ceiling (1873); West Virginia, 5% ceiling (1872); Georgia, 7% ceiling (1877); Alabama, 0.5% tax (1875); Louisiana, 1% tax (1879); Texas, 2.5% tax (1876); Arkansas, 0.5% tax (1874); Illinois, 5% ceiling (1870); Indiana, 2% tax (1881); Wisconsin, 5% ceiling (1874); Minnesota, 5% ceiling (1879); Missouri, 1% tax (1875); Nebraska, 15% ceiling (1875); Colorado, 3% ceiling (1876); California, 7% ceiling (1879).

[b]With population over 7,500.

TABLE B2

Impact of Debt Limits and Prior Debt (1870) on Local Debt, 1880

Variable	Coefficient	(SEE)	t	Sig.
Limit	−.404	(6.313)	−.064	.949
Debt pc 1870[a]	.393	(.083)	4.75	.00004

SOURCES: See Table B1.

NOTE: Dependent variable: net debt per capita, 1880, for all cities in state with populations of over 7,500. Adj. R-square = .377. Constant = 25.41.

[a]Debt for all city and town governments; population for all places over 4,000.

TABLE B3

Impact of Prior Debt and Cities (1870) on Local Debt, 1880

Variable	Coefficient	(SEE)	F	Sig.
Debt pc 1870	.361	(.070)	26.5	.00001
Cities pc 1870	−3.76	(1.05)	13	.001

SOURCES: See Table B1.

NOTE: Dependent variable: net debt per capita, 1880. The equation is based on 37 states, excluding the city of Washington, D.C., Maine (with very little debt), and Maryland (with the greatest per capita debt) as outliers. Adj. R-square = .556. Constant = 43.77.

Illinois Data Sources and Correlation Matrix of Basic Variables

Included in this appendix is Table C1, a correlation matrix for the variables used for the regression analyses of Illinois, so that readers may think in their own ways about the relationships analyzed in the text. (Cryptic abbreviations were necessary to achieve some sort of orderly visual representation; these are explained in a table note.) Some of the data in Table C1 were originally gathered in and around the Illinois constitutional convention of 1869–70, in part so that delegates could focus on fiscal issues.

Tables C2–C5 represent elaborations of and checks on the data analyses reported in the text. Throughout, outlier analyses have been run to find and remove counties that deviate enough to distort the regressions or correlations. In Table C4, tax per capita is an instrument of per capita agricultural and urban assessments and a dummy for whether or not the constitutional delegate was a Democrat. As a separate equation, the instrumental regression looks like that in Table C5.

Data in these tables come from the following sources: for delegates and their political affiliations, Illinois 1870c, 3–5, and Illinois 1870b, 176–78; for votes on the article limiting loans to railroads, Illinois 1870c, 598–99; for taxes in 1869, Illinois 1869, 86–87; for votes for and against the constitution, Illinois 1870a, 1894–95. All data are archived at the Inter-university Consortium for Political and Social Research (P.O. Box 1248, Ann Arbor, Mich. 48106). Information on political affiliation was supplemented with local histories and biographical files at the Illinois State Historical Library.

TABLE C1
Correlation Matrix
($N = 100$)

	cnrr	cnoth	cnsubs	tnrr	tnoth	tnrrsubs	ctrr	ctoth	ctsch	ctsubs	cntot	tntot	citytot	cttntot	grandtot
cnoth	-.13														
cnsubs	.17	.01													
tnrr	-.09	.26	-.08												
tnoth	-.12	-.01	-.15	-.00											
tnrrsubs	.03	.36	.09	.25	-.03										
ctrr	-.08	.09	.09	.51	-.06	-.07									
ctoth	-.13	.22	.21	.31	-.08	.13	.68								
ctsch	-.07	.14	.18	-.08	-.00	.05	.21	.75							
ctsubs	-.04	.37	.13	.24	-.08	.25	.26	.32	-.05						
cntot	.22	.78	.59	.15	-.11	.35	.10	.26	.19	.37					
tntot	-.02	.40	.03	.59	.09	.92	.13	.22	.01	.29	.33				
citytot	-.12	.22	.20	.36	-.08	.09	.79	.98	.69	.36	.26	.20			
cttntot	-.10	.38	.16	.59	-.01	.58	.64	.83	.50	.42	.37	.71	.84		
grandtot	.03	.65	.40	.49	-.06	.58	.51	.72	.45	.48	.75	.67	.72	.90	
pctvtflm	-.13	.23	-.23	.16	.11	.15	-.01	.12	.07	-.09	.03	.20	.07	.16	.14

SOURCES: For pctvtflm, Illinois 1870a, 1894–95; for all others, Illinois 1870c, statement no. 2, 100–105.

ABBREVIATIONS: cnrr, 1869 county railroad debt; cnoth, 1869 county non-railroad debt; cnsubs, 1869 county subscribed debt; tnrr, 1869 town railroad debt; tnoth, 1869 town non-railroad debt; tnrrsubs, 1869 town subscribed railroad debt; ctrr, 1869 city railroad debt; ctoth, 1869 city non-railroad debt; ctsch, 1869 city school debt (unique); ctsubs, 1869 city subscribed debt; cntot, 1869 total county debt; tntot, 1869 total town debt; citytot, 1869 total city debt; cttntot, 1869 total city and town debt combined; grandtot, 1869 total county, city, and town debt combined; pctvtflm, 1870 per capita vote for limiting debt to railroads.

NOTE: The matrix is population-weighted, with outlying Adams and Cook counties removed; weight sum = 2,132,800.

TABLE C2

Logit Regression Predicting Delegate Vote to Limit Municipal Debt
($N = 84$)

Variable	Coefficient	Std. error	t	Prob $> |t|$	Mean
For 1%					.24
Democrat	.72	.55	1.311	0.194	.39
Farmer	.88	.73	1.211	0.229	.13
Yankee	−.88	.60	−1.482	0.142	.43
Constant	−1.30	.47	−2.759	0.007	1

NOTE: Chi-square = 6.46, probability = 0.0914, log likelihood = −42.876831. This was a vote in the constitutional convention on an article limiting municipal debt to 1 percent of assessed property value. The measure failed.

TABLE C3

Robust Regression of Model in Table 2, Using Biweight Method

Source	SS	df	MS	
				$N = 101$
				$F(5, 95) - 11.55$
Model	53.40	5	10.68	Prob $> F = 0.0000$
Residual	87.81	95	.92	R-square = 0.38
				Adj R-square = 0.345
TOTAL	141.21	100	1.41	Root MSE = .961

Variable	Coefficient	Std. error	t	Prob $> |t|$	Mean
Log oddvt					1.21
Democrat	−.87	.21	−4.186	.000	.505
N towns	.10	.042	2.44	.016	2.97
Tax pc	74.32	31.00	2.40	.018	.0060
Sub. debt	−25.13	11.45	−2.20	.031	.0067
Debt pc	−26.93	15.09	−1.78	.077	.0047
Constant	1.20	.31	3.90	.000	1

ABBREVIATIONS: SS, sum of squares; df, degrees of freedom; MS, mean square; MSE, mean square error; log oddvt, log odds for vote; N towns, number of towns and cities in a country; tax pc, per capita tax; sub. debt, per capita subscribed debt; debt pc, per capita debt.

NOTE: Standard error and significance tests not valid; seven iterations; Boone Co. identified as outlying and dropped.

TABLE C4
Two-Stage Least Squares Regression of Model in Table 2, Weighted by Population

Source	SS	df	MS	$N = 100$
				$F(4, 95) = 7.17$
Model	14.83	4	3.71	Prob $> F = 0.0000$
Residual	117.19	95	1.23	R-square = 0.1123
				Adj R-square = 0.07
TOTAL	132.018	99	1.33	Root MSE = 1.110

Variable	Coefficient	Std. error	t	Prob $> \lvert t \rvert$	Mean
Log oddvt					1.50
Tax pc	288.42	88.78	3.25	0.002	.0059
Sub. debt	−37.22	15.46	−2.41	0.018	.0058
N towns	.093	.045	2.06	0.042	3.57
Debt pc	−343.00	20.86	−1.63	0.106	.0045
Constant	−.16	.49	−0.33	0.74	1

ABBREVIATIONS: See Table C3.
NOTE: Cook and Stark counties identified as outliers using Cook's D on unweighted regression and dropped.

TABLE C5
Instrument for Table C4

Source	SS	df	MS	$N = 100$
				$F(3, 96) = 15.29$
Model	.00019	3	.000064	Prob $> F = 0.0000$
Residual	.00040	96	4.2162e-06	R-square = 0.32
				Adj R-square = 0.30
TOTAL	.00060	99	6.0420e-06	Root MSE = .002

Variable	Coefficient	Std. error	t	Prob $> \lvert t \rvert$	Mean
Tax pc					.0059
Ag. ass.[a]	.027	.0055	4.890	0.000	.130
Urb. ass.[b]	.00210	.0021	.991	0.324	.116
Democrat	−.00093	.00044	−2.115	0.037	.424
Constant	.0025	.00080	3.217	0.002	1

SOURCES: For ag. ass., Illinois 1869, 72–76; for urb. ass., Illinois 1869, 77–81 (Lawrence and Macoupin counties estimated).
ABBREVIATIONS: See Table C3.
[a]Assessed value of agricultural land, including improvements, in $1,000.
[b]Assessed value of city and town lots, including improvements, in $1,000.

County Sample Selection

This short appendix gives some additional information on the counties selected for analysis in Chapter 4. The study counties were initially selected for geographical dispersion and some kind of representativeness, although that concept cannot be too rigorously applied.

There were two zero-debt counties (Calhoun and Marion) and five high-debt counties (Adams, Cook, Macoupin, Peoria, and Sangamon) in Illinois. As extremes, one of each has been included in the study: the one no-debt county with towns, Marion, with Centralia (pop. 3,109) and Salem (pop. 1,182); and the high-debt Adams, with the cities of Coatsburg, Lima, Mendon, and Quincy.

From the middle of the pack, I analyzed the debt in the year of the new constitution, when limitations were put into effect. To find those middle towns and cities, I regressed the difference in city and town debt predicted by number of towns and their population and 1869 debt, excluding Cook County (see Table D2).

Twelve counties proved to be potential median counties. All have easily predicted changes for the 1869–70 period based on residuals drawn from the regression of change in debt by 1869 debt and population in cities and towns. Three counties had residuals of less than $4,000: Boone, Monroe, and Richland. Nine counties had residuals of less than $10,000 and more than $4,000: Clinton, Cumberland, Effingham, Fulton, Gallatin, Jersey, Logan, Massac, and Schulyer. From these I selected geographically dispersed Cumberland, Fulton, and Gallatin (supplemented with Massac, because each had few towns, and sources for both were thin). The six counties selected thus far did not include either a northern county or a county that was very supportive of a constitutional limit; for this I selected DeKalb, an agricultural county with only two towns (and, as it turned out, not much else). In addition to meeting the original criteria for dispersion, none of the selected counties were in the same legislative or convention district or had non-farmer noes in the convention.

TABLE D1
Study Counties

County	Supported debt limit	Newspaper	County seat	1870 pop.	Selection rationale
Adams	no	*Quincy Herald, Quincy Whig*	Quincy	24,052	high debt
Cumberland	no	*Toledo Democrat*	Majority Pt./ Toledo	township	predictable debt
DeKalb	yes	*DeKalb County News*	Sycamore	2,852	geography
Fulton	no	*Fulton County Ledger*	Lewistown	township	predictable debt
Gallatin	no	*Shawneetown News*	Shawneetown	1,309	predictable debt
Massac[a]	yes				
Marion	yes	*Centralia Sentinel*	Salem	township	low debt

[a] A supplement to Gallatin.

TABLE D2
Regression for Identifying Typical Illinois Counties

Source	SS	df	MS	
				$N = 101$
				$F(3, 97) = 34.65$
Model	637206.541	3	212402.18	Prob > F = .00
Residual	594554.995	97	6129.43293	R-square = .52
				Adj R-square = .50
TOTAL	1231761.54	100	12317.6154	Root MSE = 78.29

Variable	Coefficient	Std. error	t	Prob > $|t|$	Mean
Debt change					23.92
Urban pop.	−.02	.002	−6.11	.000	4624.76
1869 debt	.41	.042	9.77	.000	118.59
N towns	.39	4.04	.098	.922	2.95
Constant	42.24	12.57	3.36	.001	1

SOURCES: See Table C1.
ABBREVIATIONS: SS, sum of squares; df, degrees of freedom; MS, mean square; MSE, mean square error; N towns, number of towns and cities in a county.

Illinois-Originated Cases on Debt, 1859–96

This lists all reported cases indexed on municipal debt-related issues. Those that went to federal courts are noted as (U.S.); if not so noted, the case never went beyond the Illinois courts. All cases are from those in *Century Edition of the American Digest: A Complete Digest of all Reported Cases from the Earliest Time to 1897* (1658–1896), vol. 36 (West Publishing: St. Paul, 1902) and are found under various headings related to municipal corporations. Only reported cases are included. For a discussion of contemporary bias in reported cases, see Siegelman and Donohue 1990.

1859

People v. Tazewell County, 22 Ill. (12 Peck) 47.
Robertson v. City of Rockford, 21 Ill. (11 Peck) 451.

1860

Johnson v. Stark County, 24 Ill. 75.
Perkins v. Lewis, 24 Ill. 208.

1861

Butler v. Dunham, 27 Ill. 474.
City of Quincy v. Warfield, 25 Ill. (15 Peck) 317, 79 Am. Dec. 330.

1862

No cases.

1863

City of Pekin v. Reynolds, 31 Ill. 529, 83 Am. Dec. 244.

1864

Town of Keithsburg v. Frick, 34 Ill. 405.

1865

No cases.

1866

Harvey v. Town of Olney, 42 Ill. 336.

1867

No cases.

1868

City of Galena v. Corwith, 48 Ill. 423, 95 Am. Dec. 557.

1869

People v. City Council of Cairo, 50 Ill. 154.

1870

People v. Canty, 55 Ill. 33.
People v. Dutcher, 56 Ill. 144.
Wider v. City of East St. Louis, 55 Ill. 133.
City of Chicago v. People, 56 Ill. 327.

1871

Village of Lockport v. Gaylord, 61 Ill. 276.
Force v. Town of Batavia, 61 Ill. 99.
Wiley v. Silliman, 62 Ill. 170.
Sherlock v. Village of Winnetka, 59 Ill. 389.
Chicago, Danville & Vincennes Railroad v. Smith, 62 Ill. 268, 14 Am. Rep.
    99.

1872

(U.S.) St. Joseph Township v. Rogers, 83 U.S. (16 Wall.) 644, 21 L. Ed. 328.
Bissell v. City of Kankakee, 64 Ill. 249, 21 Am. Pep. 554 (following Marsh v.
    Fullerton County [1870] 10 Wall. 676, 19 L. Ed. 1040).
Schall v. Bowman, 62 Ill. 321.
Richards v. Donagho, 66 Ill. 73.
Town of Big Grove v. Wells, 65 Ill. 263.
McWhorter v. People, 65 Ill. 290.
People v. Cline, 63 Ill. 394.

1873

(U.S.) Marcy v. Town of Ohio, F. Cas. 9457, affirming Id. (1873) 85 U.S.
    (18 Wall.) 522, 21 L. Ed. 813.

People v. Town of Harp, 67 Ill. 62.
People v. Town of Santa Anna, 67 Ill. 57.
People v. Town of Laenna, 67 Ill. 65.
Sherlock v. Village of Winnetka, 68 Ill. 530.
Decker v. Hughes, 68 Ill. 33.
Ryan v. Lynch, 68 Ill. 160.
Flack v. Hughes, 67 Ill. 384.

1874

City of Kinmundy v. Mahan, 72 Ill. 462.
Chicago and Iowa Railroad v. Pinckney, 74 Ill. 277.

1875

(U.S.) Balcheller v. Town of Mascoutah, Fed. Cas. No. 792.
Burr v. City of Carbondale, 76 Ill. 455.
Mason v. City of Shawneetown, 77 Ill. 533.
Cairo & St. Louis Railroad v. City of Sparta, 77 Ill. 505.
People v. Brislin, 80 Ill. 423.

1876

(U.S.) Town of South Ottawa v. Perkins, 94 U.S. 260, 24 L. Ed. 154.
Town of Eagle v. Kohn, 84 Ill. 292.
Town of Middleport v. Aetna Life Insurance, 82 Ill. 562.
People v. Lippincott, 81 Ill. 193.

1877

(U.S.) County of Henry v. Nicolay, 95 U.S. 619.
(U.S.) Warren County v. Marcy, 97 U.S. 96, 24 L. Ed. 977.
City of Springfield v. Edwards, 84 Ill. 626.
Quincy, Missouri & Pacific Railroad v. Morris, 84 Ill. 410.
Law v. People, 87 Ill. 385.
Shawneetown v. Baker, 85 Ill. 563.
Barnes v. Town of Lacon, 84 Ill. 461.
Brauns v. Town of Peoria, 82 Ill. 11.
Village of Kansas v. Juntgen, 84 Ill. 360.

1878

(U.S.) Merriwether v. Saline County, Fed. Cas. No. 9485 (5 Dill. 265).
(U.S.) Hackett v. City of Ottawa, 99 U.S. 86, 25 L. Ed. 363.
(U.S.) Nauvoo v. Ritter, 97 U.S. 389, 24 L. Ed. 1050.
Richard County v. People, 3 Ill. App. (3 Bradw.) 210.
Wright v. Bishop, 88 Ill. 302.

Williams v. Town of Roberts, 88 Ill. 11.
Fuller v. Heath, 1 Ill. App. (1 Bradw.) 118.
Fuller v. Heath, 89 Ill. 296.
Barrett v. City of St. Louis, 89 Ill. 175.
South Park Commissioners v. Dunlevy, 91 Ill. 49.
Fuller v. City of Chicago, 89 Ill. 282.
People v. Town of Waynesville, 88 Ill. 469.
Crane v. City of Urbana, 2 Ill. App. (2 Bradw.) 559.

1879

(U.S.) Leslie v. Urbana, Fed. Cas. No. 8,276 (8 Biss. 435).
(U.S.) Town of Roberts v. Bolles, 101 U.S. 119, 25 L. Ed. 880 (distinguish-
   ing Williams v. Town of Roberts [1878] 88 Ill. 11).
Parker v. Smith, 3 Ill. App. (3 Bradw.) 356.
Gaddis v. Richland County, 92 Ill. 119.
Lippincott v. Town of Pana, 92 Ill. 24, affirming Id. (1877), 2 Ill. App.
   466.
People v. Town Clerk of Barnett, 91 Ill. 422.
Thatcher v. People, 93 Ill. 240.
People v. Jackson County, 92 Ill. 441.
Niantic Savings Bank v. Town of Douglas, 5 Ill. 579.
City of Cairo v. Allen, 3 Ill. App. (3 Bradw.) 398.
Pitzman v. Village of Freeburg, 92 Ill. 111.

1880

(U.S.) Portsmouth Savings Bank v. City of Springfield, (C.C.) 4 Fed. 276.
(U.S.) Buchanan v. Litchfield, 102 U.S. 278, 26 L. Ed. 138.
(U.S.) Harter Township v. Kernochan, 103 U.S. 563, 26 L. Ed. 411.
Town of Prairie v. Lloyd, 97 Ill. 179.
Town of Windsor v. Hallett, 97 Ill. 204.
Douglas v. Niantic Savings Bank, 97 Ill. 228.
Chicago v. Carqueville Lithographing, 6 Ill. App. 560.
Board of Education v. Taft, 7 Ill. App. 571.

1881

(U.S.) Carey v. City of Ottawa, (C.C.) 8 Fed. 199.
(U.S.) Ottawa v. First National Bank of Portsmouth, 105 U.S. 342, 26 L. Ed.
   1127.
(U.S.) Clay County v. Society for Savings, 104 U.S. 579, 26 L. Ed. 856.
City of East St. Louis v. East St. Louis Gaslight and Coke, 98 Ill. 415, 38 Am.
   Rep. 97.

Water Commissioners v. Hall, 98 Ill. 371.
Chicago, Burlington & Quincy Railway v. City of Aurora, 99 Ill. 205.
City of East St. Louis v. Maxwell, 99 Ill. 439.

1882

(U.S.) Town of Pana v. Bowler, 107 U.S. 529, 2 S. Ct. 704, 27 L. Ed. 424.
(U.S.) City of Quincy v. Cooke, 107 U.S. 549, 2 S. Ct. 614, 27 L. Ed. 549.
City of East St. Louis v. Trustees of Schools, 102 Ill. 489, 40 Am. Rep. 606.
Prince v. City of Quincy, 105 Ill. 138, 44 Am. Rep. 785; (1883) Prince v. City
    of Quincy, 105 Ill. 215.

1883

(U.S.) Town of Aurora v. Auditor of State, (C.C.) 15 F. 843.
(U.S.) City of Ottawa v. Carey, 108 U.S. 110, 1 S. Ct., 2 S. Ct. 361, L. Ed. 669.
City of East St. Louis v. Underwood, 105 Ill. 308.

1884

(U.S.) City of Jonesboro v. Cairo & St. Louis Railroad, 110 U.S. 192, 4 S. Ct.
    67, 28 L. Ed. 116.
Wade v. Town of La Moille, 112 Ill. 79.
People v. Town of Bishop, 111 Ill. 124, 53 Am. Rep. 605.
Wade v. Town of La Moille, 112 Ill. 79.

1885

Jacksonville Railway v. City of Jacksonville, 114 Ill. 562, 2 N.E. 478.
Mather v. City of Ottawa, 114 Ill. 659, 3 N.E. 216.
Dutton v. City of Aurora, 114 Ill. 138, 28 N.E. 461.

1886

(U.S.) Town of Oregon v. Jennings, 119 U.S. 74, 7 S. Ct. 124, 30 L. Ed. 323.
Harmon v. Auditor of Public Accounts, 22 Ill. App. 129, affirmed (1887),
    123 Ill. 122, 13 N.E. 161, 5 Am. St. Rep. 502.
Richeson v. People, 115 Ill. 450, 5 N.E. 121.
Village of Sheridan v. Hibbard, 19 Ill. App. (19 Bradw.) 421, affirmed
    (1887) 119 Ill. 307, 9 N.E. 901.

1887

(U.S.) Town of Concord v. Robinson, 121 U.S. 165, 7 S. Ct. 937, 30 L. Ed.
    885.
Town of Aurora v. Chicago, Burlington & Quincy Railroad, 119 Ill. 246, 10
    N.E. 27.

1888

(U.S.) German Savings Bank v. Franklin County, 128 U.S. 526, 9 S. Ct. 159, 32 L. Ed. 519.
Culbertson v. City of Fulton, 127 Ill. 30, 18 N.E. 781.
Dehm v. City of Havana, 28 Ill. App. 520.
Prince v. City of Quincy, 28 Ill. App. 490, affirmed (1889) 128 Ill. 443, 21 N.E. 768.
City of East St. Louis v. Flannigan, 26 Ill. App. 449.

1889

(U.S.) Town of Elmswood v. Dows, 136 U.S. 651, 10 S. Ct. 1074, 34 L. Ed. 555; (1888) Id. (C.C.) 34 F. 114.
Eddy v. People, 127 Ill. 428, 20 N.E. 83.
Carlyle Water, Light and Power v. City of Carlyle, 31 Ill. App. 325.
Prince v. City of Quincy, 128 Ill. 443, 21 N.E. 768, affirming (1888) 28 Ill. App. 490.

1890

(U.S.) Illinois G. T. Railway v. Wade, 140 U.S. 65, 70, 11 S. Ct. 709, 35 L. Ed. 342.
(U.S.) City of East St. Louis v. United States, 110 U.S. 321, 4 S. Ct. 21, 28 L. Ed. 162.
Williams v. People, 132 Ill. 574, 24 N.E. 647.
Norton v. City of East St. Louis, 36 Ill. App. 171.
City of East St. Louis v. Flannigan, 34 Ill. App. 596.
Town of Mt. Morris v. Williams, 38 Ill. App. 401 (following City of Pekin v. Reynolds [1863] 31 Ill. 529, 83 Am. Dec. 244).
Casey v. People, 132 Ill. 546, 24 N.E. 570.

1891

Hackman v. Village of Staunton, 42 Ill. App. 409.
People v. Getzendaner, 137 Ill. 234, 34 N.E. 297.
Town of Bloomington v. Lillard, 39 Ill. App. 616.

1892

East St. Louis Gaslight and Coke v. City of East St. Louis, 45 Ill. App. 591.
Samson v. People, 141 Ill. 17, 30 N.E. 781.
Choisser v. People, 140 Ill. 21, 29 N.E. 546.

1893

(U.S.) City of Cairo v. Zane, 149 U.S. 122, 13 S. Ct. 803, 37 L. Ed. 673.
Griswold v. City of East St. Louis, 47 Ill. App. 480.

1894

Hutchinson v. Self, 153 Ill. 542, 39 N.E. 27.

People v. Superior Court of Cook County, 55 Ill. App. 376.

1895

Directors of Chicago Public Library v. Arnold, 60 Ill. App. 328.

City of Fulton v. Northern Illinois College, 158 Ill. 333, 42 N.E. 138, affirming (1894) 56 Ill. App. 372.

1896

(U.S.) Graves v. Saline County, 161 U.S. 359, 16 S. Ct. 526, 40 L. Ed. 732.

(U.S.) Wesson v. Saline County, 73 F. 917, 20 C.C.A. 227 (following City of Evansville v. Dennett [1896] 161 U.S. 434, 16 S. Ct. 613, 40 L. Ed. 760).

(U.S.) Ashman v. Pulaski County, 73 F. 927, 20 C.C.A. 232.

Kane v. City of Charleston, 161 Ill. 179, 43 N.E. 611.

Reference Matter

Notes

INTRODUCTION

1. Almost all scholars have neglected the fiscal role of redevelopment agencies, which in the past twenty years have become one of the most significant entities shaping the look of the city. For an outstanding exception, see Young 1990.

2. Thomas Bender cites this case in what is arguably *the* study of American urban culture—naturally dealing with New York City (Bender 1987, 177).

3. This assertion sets my analysis off, therefore, from those of a range of scholars who have unlocked the urban puzzle. For example, in her study of Chicago finance and politics in the antebellum period, Robin Einhorn emphasizes how direct assessment—that is, property owners paying sidewalk contractors, for example, directly—kept a portion of city infrastructural payments off the budget. She makes these payments a key to understanding the city's finances and its relationship to property. I am reluctant to emphasize these so much; although unmonetized, they cannot have been nearly the equivalent of another common device in Illinois, a requirement that town-dwelling men spend two or three days a year laboring on the roads.

CHAPTER 1

1. Lack of interest on the part of economists has contributed to the failure adequately to investigate local finance. For instance, only recently, over two decades after the major article examining the economics of nineteenth-century local government expenditure (which does not actually measure expenditures but estimates them), has a new project been

launched to measure such expenditures (Davis and Legler 1966; Legler, Sylla, and Wallis 1986).

CHAPTER 2

1. This chapter is a version of an essay published in *The Politics of Urban Fiscal Policy*, edited by Sally Ward and Terrence J. McDonald (Beverly Hills, Calif.: Sage, 1984), 125–59.

2. The history of state debts and their repudiations is the topic of at least one book (McGrane 1935), yet nowhere does municipal or other local governmental debt enter the discussion. Because of their high international visibility, state debts have become textbook material, while local ones have been forgotten.

3. See, for example, Monkkonen 1981a and 1981c, where I assert that a change in the level of a series of drunkenness arrests reflected the impact of World War II.

4. McCleary and Hay use a plot of 1,000 successive coin flips to exemplify the notion: while summing to zero, the additive value of a succession of coin flips drifts upward or downward for long periods. Without other knowledge, one might well read the plot as containing a caused set of trends (McCleary and Hay 1980, 36–45).

CHAPTER 3

1. See Cornelius 1980, 56–84, for an excellent summary of the convention.

2. The parallels between the New York constitutional issues and those of Illinois 30 years later are remarkable: New Yorkers took on state debt, and 30 years later Illinoisans turned to local debt. The issue of racial suffrage came up in each case, and both new constitutions mandated considerable liberalization. There is no link between these issues, except that increased suffrage is an aspect of the rationalized liberal state, while severe fiscal limitation is ordinarily conceptualized as an anti-state action.

3. See Ray Gunn (1988), who characterizes this change as democratization. He stresses the downward shift to the county, but completely ignores municipal governments. However, Clifford Blunk has pointed out that the limitations imposed on state government in the 1840s were followed by the movement to limit local government in the 1870s (Blunk 1926).

4. Since there is virtually no correlation between railroad debt and the vote to limit it, the idea that these debt-free counties wished to rein in counties liable for railroad debt must be rejected.

5. Counties with a high debt/property ratio included Adams, 14 percent; Alexander, 12 percent; Cook, 16 percent; Kendall, 7 percent; Marshall, 8 percent; Peoria, 13 percent; Piatt, 9 percent; Sangamon, 9 percent; and Stark, 15 percent.

6. Note in addition that the correlation matrix of all debt measures (see Table C1) shows very little intercorrelation. More important, they show virtually no bivariate relationship between voting against railroad debt and existing local debt.

7. The difference between opposition and support probabilities is owing to the abstentions. McCormick 1986 (210–11) sums up recent research on the national level that finds no partisan differences on economic development issues. Shade 1972, on the other hand, sees the Democrats' antebellum culture as continuing after the Civil War, as they "combined enthusiasm for cultural pluralism with vicious antiblack racism. . . . They emphasized states' rights and respect for local institutions . . . [but the Democrats feared] commercialization, an economic indicator of cultural domination by Yankee-Protestant values and habits" (253–54).

8. The convention took a vote on a related issue, a proposal to limit municipal debt to 1 percent of the assessed value of a municipality. The issue elicited similar partisanship, even though not all of the voters were the same. The coefficient for Democrats was -3.64 (with the highest t value, as in Table 1), again demonstrating the strong Democratic opposition to this very constrictive proposal. See regression in Table C2.

9. In the analyses that follow, I also ran preliminary tests on the impact of voter turnout, but it made no meaningful difference.

10. I also estimated this model using robust regression, included in Table C3, and by using a two-stage least squares or instrumental variable version in Table C4.

11. Log odds (sometimes called logit) equal the natural log (a county's percentage vote divided by 100 minus the county's percentage vote).

12. See Table C4 for a two-stage least squares version of this analysis, where tax is estimated as an instrumental variable of assessed property value and a dummy for the convention delegate's partisan identification as a Democrat. The coefficients and shape of this analysis conform to the one presented here in the text.

CHAPTER 4

1. Cumberland County was my original south central Illinois selection. It had the poorest farmland of any of the study counties, was represented by a Democrat in the convention, and voted in favor of the railroad limit by a

slim 55 percent. The county remains highly rural today. The Illinois Central passed through the village of Neoga in the northwest corner of the county, bringing with it the early benefits of rail service with no special effort on the county's part. Unfortunately, its extant newspapers and local histories are too fragmentary to be of much use, and as a study county, it had to be replaced by neighboring Marion.

2. Quincy's location, for example, enabled it "to compete successfully with such cities as Pittsburgh, Cincinnati and St. Louis" (Redmond 1869, 19–20).

3. These were drawn from *Municipal Corporations — Naval Officers*, vol. 36 of the *Century Edition of the American Digest* (1902), using all subject headings that could be construed as relevant to finance: sections 3, 13, 14, and 15. One hundred five cases were Illinois Supreme Court decisions, and 32 were federal. This approach to the cases was suggested to me by Christine Rosen's forthcoming study of smoke abatement ordinances. Appendix E contains citations of all of these cases.

4. Who were the bondholders? The only clue we have is in the cases where we see them bringing suit against defaulters, and these were an unusual bunch, often creditors who had bought up defaulted bonds on speculation, hoping for a settlement at some value over their investment. There is evidence in the cases of Ottawa and Watertown (see Chapter 5) that investors included wealthy locals, but we cannot assess how representative such investors were. It may well be that, like the speculators, they sued for repayment because of their knowledge of local affairs.

5. According to testimony, 140 to 150 residents ordinarily voted. See Illinois State Archives, Miscellaneous Case Files, RS 901.1, Supreme Court, Roll 30-1840, *People v. Town of Bishop*, 41.

6. Ibid., 24.

7. Ottawa 50 years later became home to the Radium Dial Company, an enterprise that was responsible for the cancer deaths of workers in the 1920s and 1930s and that later spawned the infamous Radium Chemical Company of Queens, the largest single-point polluter with radioactive material in U.S. history (*New York Times*, September 10, 1989, section 1, 17).

8. *Ottawa v. Carey*, 108 U.S. 110–24 (1884); quotation at 122. Parts of the following section are from Monkkonen 1994.

9. *Ottawa v. Carey*, 108 U.S. 110–24 (1884), 121.

10. Newspaper citation from the Cole Notes, Illinois Historical Survey. My thanks to John Hoffman for this citation.

CHAPTER 5

1. Laura Brockington 1983 shows, for example, how Democrats promoted the "race riot" to expel the Republican and Populist government of Wilmington, N.C.

2. James D. Williams, "Duluth Apologizes After 71 Years," *Crisis* 99 (January 1992): 21; M. V. Andrews, "Take Duluth . . . Please," *Plastic and Reconstructive Surgery* 92 (October 1993): 941–42; Kjell Rodne, "Duluth's Revival," *Public Management* 73 (March 1991): 8.

3. See Abbott 1981 for an analysis of the rhetoric of town boosters.

4. Sigafoos 1979, 121–23, finds "evidence of this strong relationship between local politics and business," although members of the elite seldom actually ran for office.

5. See Fine 1975, chaps. 11–12, for an account of the politics of Detroit in this troubled era.

6. Fine 1975, 355–57, has a detailed account of the Associations for Tax Reduction's campaign for a limited city budget. His account emphasizes the conservative nature of the coalition, dominated by the real estate industry, thereby contradicting the Real Estate Board's stand against the limited budget.

CONCLUSION

1. See, for example, the imaginative promotion of Duluth's rosy future in Duluth Energy Resource Center 1986.

2. Note that in all of these events and relationships, a kind of passive action is unavailable to county and municipal governments: both the federal and state governments may authorize action at the next lower level of government without seeming to build the power of the authorizing body, as when the federal government has mandated local actions in the 1980s and 1990s under the guise of federalism.

3. Jon Teaford (1975; 1979; 1984) and Hendrik Hartog (1979) have demonstrated that for the most part state governments gave cities the legislation they wanted. Teaford 1984 shows how legislative committees dealing with cities were usually in fact staffed with urban legislators.

4. Southern states did not exactly follow this pattern; see the contrast drawn in Pease and Pease 1985.

5. "Local governmental responsibility, family responsibility, and legal settlement — the three principles expressed in the English Poor Law — were transplanted some 250 years later to a new Midwestern American terri-

tory" (McClure 1968, 7). Breckenridge 1939, 9–13, discusses the North-west Territory's welfare provision of 1795.

6. There is at least one case when the relationship must have been clear: in the 1950s, Burlington, Vermont, replaced its poor farm with an elementary school (Hoffbeck 1989, 235).

7. Some of what follows derives from Eric H. Monkkonen, "What Urban Crisis? An Historian's Point of View," *Urban Affairs Quarterly* 20 (June 1985): 429–47.

8. The consequence of *Serrano v. Priest* (1971), which equalized spending per student across the state. See California Council on Intergovernmental Relations 1972.

Works Cited

Abbott, Carl. 1981. *Boosters and Businessmen: Popular Economic Thought and Urban Growth in the Antebellum Middle West.* Westport, Conn.: Greenwood Press.

Advisory Commission on Intergovernmental Relations. 1961 (Sept.). *State Constitutional and Statutory Restrictions on Local Taxing Powers.* Washington, D.C.: Advisory Commission on Intergovernmental Relations.

———. 1962 (Oct.). *State Constitutional and Statutory Restrictions on Local Government Debt.* Washington, D.C.: Advisory Commission on Intergovernmental Relations.

Alcaly, R. E., and D. Mermelstein, eds. 1977. *The Fiscal Crisis of American Cities: Essays on the Political Economy of Urban America with Special Reference to New York.* New York: Vintage Books.

Amdursky, Robert S., and Clayton P. Gillette. 1992. *Municipal Debt Finance Law: Theory and Practice.* Boston: Little, Brown.

Anderson, Alan. 1977. *The Origin and Resolution of an Urban Crisis: Baltimore, 1890–1930.* Baltimore, Md.: Johns Hopkins Univ. Press.

Anthony, Elliott. 1891. *The Constitutional History of Illinois.* Chicago: Chicago Legal News Print.

Argersinger, Peter H. 1985–86. "New Perspectives on Election Fraud in the Gilded Age." *Political Science Quarterly* 100: 669–88.

Aronson, J. Richard, and Eli Schwartz, eds. 1975. *Management Policies in Local Government Finance.* Washington, D.C.: International City Management Association.

Asbury, Henry. 1882. *Reminiscences of Quincy, Illinois.* Quincy, Ill.: D. Wilcox & Sons.

Barron, Hal S. 1989. "And the Crooked Shall Be Made Straight: Public Road Administration and the Decline of Localism in the Rural North, 1870–1930." *Journal of Social History* 26: 81–104.

Baxter, Maurice G. 1957. *Orville H. Browning: Lincoln's Friend and Critic.* Bloomington: Indiana Univ. Press.

Beadie, Nancy E. 1989. "Defining the Public: Congregation, Commerce, and Social Economy in the Formation of the Educational System, 1790–1840." Ph.D. diss., Syracuse Univ.

Beito, David T. 1989. *Taxpayers in Revolt: Tax Resistance During the Depression.* Chapel Hill: Univ. of North Carolina Press.

Bender, Thomas. 1987. *New York Intellect: A History of Intellectual Life in New York City from 1750 to the Beginnings of Our Own Time.* New York: Knopf.

Benson, G. C. S., S. Benson, H. McClelland, and P. Thompson. 1965. *The American Property Tax: Its History, Administration, and Economic Impact.* Claremont, Calif.: College Press.

Betters, Paul V. 1933[?]. *Municipal Finance Problems and Proposals for Federal Legislation.* Chicago: American Municipal Association.

——. 1936a. *Cities and the 1936 Congress.* Washington, D.C.: U.S. Conference of Mayors.

——. 1936b. *Recent Federal City Relations.* Washington, D.C.: U.S. Conference of Mayors.

Bird, Frederick L. 1931. *The Present Financial Status of 135 Cities in the United States and Canada.* New York: National Municipal League.

——. 1935. *The Municipal Debt Load in 1935: Cities of over 50,000 Population.* New York: Dun & Bradstreet.

Bishop, Ward L. 1928. "An Economic Analysis of the Constitutional Restrictions on Municipal Indebtedness in Illinois." *University of Illinois Studies in the Social Sciences* 16, no. 1. Urbana: Univ. of Illinois Press.

Blunk, Clifford L. M. 1926. "Constitutional Restrictions on Public Indebtedness in Illinois." Master's thesis, Univ. of Illinois.

Breckenridge, Sophonisba P. 1939. *The Illinois Poor Law and Its Administration.* Chicago: Univ. of Chicago Press.

Brockington, Laura A. 1983. "Redeeming North Carolina: The Wilmington Race Riot of November 1898." Honors thesis, Univ. of California, Los Angeles.

Brownson, Howard G. 1915. "History of the Illinois Central Railroad to 1870." *University of Illinois Studies in the Social Sciences* 1, nos. 3 (Sept.) and 4 (Dec.). Urbana: Univ. of Illinois Press.

Burton, Clarence M. 1917. *History of Detroit, 1780–1850: Financial and Commercial Detroit.* Detroit, Mich.: n.p.

California Council on Intergovernmental Relations. 1972. *Serrano v. Priest: The Decision, the Implications and the Alternatives for Funding.* Sacramento: California Council on Intergovernmental Relations.

Capers, Gerald M., Jr. 1939. *The Biography of a River Town: Memphis: Its Heroic Age*. Chapel Hill: Univ. of North Carolina Press.

Carleton, Mark T. 1971. *Politics and Punishment: The History of the Louisiana State Penal System*. Baton Rouge: Louisiana State Univ. Press.

Carr, Kathryn Joyce. 1987. "Belleville and Galesburg: Decision-Making and Community Political Culture on the Illinois Frontier." Ph.D. diss., Univ. of Chicago.

Citrin, J., and F. Levy. 1981. "From 13 to 4 and Beyond: The Political Meaning of the Ongoing Tax Revolt in California." In *The Property Tax Revolt: The Case of Proposition 13*, ed. G. G. Kaufman and K. T. Rosen, 1–26. Cambridge, Mass.: Ballinger.

Clotfelter, Charles. 1973. "Memphis Business Leadership and the Politics of Fiscal Crisis." *West Tennessee Historical Society Papers* 27: 33–49.

Cochran, Thomas C. 1948. "The 'Presidential Synthesis' in American History." *American Historical Review* 52 (July): 748–59.

Cole, Arthur C. 1919. *The Era of the Civil War, 1848–1870*. Springfield: Illinois Centennial Commission.

Collins, William H., and Cicero F. Perry. 1905. *Past and Present of the City of Quincy and Adams County, Illinois*. Chicago: S. J. Clarke.

Conot, Robert. 1974. *American Odyssey*. New York: Morrow.

Conzen, Michael P. 1987. *Focus on Ottawa: A Historical and Geographical Survey of Ottawa, Illinois, in the Twentieth Century*. Chicago: Univ. of Chicago Committee on Geographical Studies.

Cooley, James E. 1925. *Recollections of Early Days in Duluth*. Duluth, Minn.: published by author.

Cornelius, Janet. 1980. *Constitution Making in Illinois, 1818–1870*. Chicago: Univ. of Illinois Press.

A Courthouse Conservation Handbook. 1976. Washington, D.C.: Preservation Press.

Davis, Lance, and John Legler. 1966. "The Government in the American Economy, 1815–1902: A Quantitative Study." *Journal of Economic History* 26: 514–52.

Dillon, John F. 1872. *Treatise on the Law of Municipal Corporations*. Chicago: J. Cockroft.

Directory, Charter and Ordinances of the City of Shawneetown. 1872. Shawneetown, Ill.

Duluth Energy Resource Center. 1986. *Resettling Duluth*. Duluth, Minn.: Duluth Energy Resource Center.

Einhorn, Robin Leigh. 1988. "Before the Machine: Municipal Government in Chicago, 1833–1872." Ph.D. diss., Univ. of Chicago.

Elazar, Daniel J. 1962. *The American Partnership: Intergovernmental Coopera-*

tion in the Nineteenth-Century United States. Chicago: Univ. of Chicago Press.

———. 1987. *Building Cities in America: Urbanization and Suburbanization in a Frontier Society.* Lanham, Md.: Hamilton Press.

Fairman, Charles. 1971. *History of the Supreme Court of the United States: Reconstruction and Reunion, 1864–88.* Vol. 6. New York: Macmillan.

Feagin, Joe R. 1988. *Free Enterprise City: Houston in Political-Economic Perspective.* New Brunswick, N.J.: Rutgers Univ. Press.

Fesler, James W. 1967. *The Fifty States and Their Local Governments.* New York: Knopf.

Fine, Sidney. 1975. *Frank Murphy: The Detroit Years.* Ann Arbor: Univ. of Michigan Press.

Fisher, Glenn W., and Robert P. Fairbanks. 1968. *Illinois Municipal Finance: A Financial and Economic Analysis.* Urbana: Univ. of Illinois Press.

Friedman, Lawrence M. 1973. *A History of American Law.* New York: Simon & Schuster.

———. 1981. "History, Social Policy, and Criminal Justice." In *Social History and Social Policy,* ed. D. Rothman and S. Wheeler, 203–35. New York: Academic Press.

Frug, Gerald E. 1980. "The City as Legal Concept." *Harvard Law Review* 93: 1059–154.

Fuchs, Ester R. 1992. *Mayors and Money: Fiscal Policy in New York and Chicago.* Chicago: Univ. of Chicago Press.

Galambos, Louis. 1983. "Technology, Political Economy, and Professional Organization: Central Themes of the Organizational Synthesis." *Business History Review* 57 (Mar.): 471–93.

Gelfand, Mark I. 1975. *A Nation of Cities: The Federal Government and Urban America, 1933–1965.* New York: Oxford Univ. Press.

Gelfand, M. David. 1979. "Seeking Local Government Financial Integrity Through Debt Ceilings, Tax Limits, and Expenditure Limits: The New York City Fiscal Crisis, the Taxpayer Revolt, and Beyond." *Minnesota Law Review* 63 (Apr.): 545–608.

Gere, Edwin A. 1982. "Dillon's Rule and the Cooley Doctrine: Reflections of the Political Culture." *Journal of Urban History* 8: 271–91.

Gunn, Ray L. 1988. *The Decline of Authority: Public Economic Policy and Political Development in New York, 1800–1860.* Ithaca, N.Y.: Cornell Univ. Press.

Hansen, Stephen L. 1980. *The Making of the Third Party System: Voters and Parties in Illinois, 1850–1876.* Ann Arbor: Univ. of Michigan Press.

Hardy, Bruce A. 1977. "American Privatism and the Urban Fiscal Crisis of the Interwar Years: A Financial Study of the Cities of New York,

Chicago, Philadelphia, Detroit, and Boston, 1915–1945." Ph.D. diss., Wayne State Univ.

Hartog, Hendrik. 1979. "Because All the World Was Not New York City: Governance, Property Rights, and the State in the Changing Definition of a Corporation, 1730–1860." *Buffalo Law Review* 28: 91–109.

Heckman, Charles A. 1988. "Establishing the Basis for Local Financing of American Railroad Construction in the Nineteenth Century: From *City of Bridgeport v. The Housatonic Railroad Company* to *Gelpcke v. City of Dubuque.*" *American Journal of Legal History* 32: 236–64.

Hemple, George F. 1971. *The Postwar Quality of State and Municipal Debt.* New York: National Bureau of Economic Research.

Hillhouse, Arthur M. 1935. *Defaulted Municipal Bonds, 1830–1930.* Chicago: Municipal Finance Officers' Association.

———. 1936. *Municipal Bonds: A Century of Experience.* New York: Prentice-Hall.

Hobsbawm, Eric, and George Rude. 1975. *Captain Swing: A Social History of the Great English Agricultural Uprising of 1830.* New York: Norton.

Hoffbeck, Steven R. 1989. " 'Remember the Poor' (Galatians 2:10): Poor Farms in Vermont." *Vermont History* 57: 226–40.

Hoffman, J. 1983. "Urban Squeeze Plays: New York City Crises of the 1930s and 1970s." *Radical Review of Political Economics* 12: 29–57.

Holli, Melvin, ed. *Detroit.* New York: Franklin Watts, 1976.

Horwitz, A. B. C. 1939. *Land Platting in Duluth, Minnesota, 1856–1939.* Duluth, Minn.: Works Project Administration.

Hughes, T. P. 1969–71. "1878 Yellow Fever Epidemic in Memphis and Shelby County, Tennessee." *Ansearchin News* 16–18.

Hume, John F. 1884. "Are We a Nation of Rascals?" *North American Review* (Aug.): 127–44.

Hurst, James Willard. [1956] 1967. *Law and the Conditions of Freedom in the Nineteenth-Century United States.* Reprint. Madison: Univ. of Wisconsin Press.

Illinois. 1840. *Laws of the State of Illinois.* Springfield.

———. 1863. *Private Laws of the State of Illinois.* Springfield.

———. 1869. *Annual Report of the Auditor of Public Accounts.* Springfield, Dec. 15.

———. 1870a. *Debates and Proceedings of the Constitutional Convention.* Springfield.

———. 1870b. *The Illinois Hand-Book of Information for the Year 1870.* Springfield.

———. 1870c. *Journal of the Constitutional Convention of the State of Illinois.* Springfield.

———. 1926. *Blue Book of State of Illinois, 1925–1926.* Springfield.

Illinois Auditor of Public Accounts. 1872. *Biennial Report of the Auditor of Public Accounts.* Springfield.

———. 1874. *Biennial Report of the Auditor of Public Accounts.* Springfield.

Illinois State Archives. Miscellaneous Case Files RS 901.1. Supreme Court. Roll 30-1841.

Iowa. 1857. *Constitution.* Art. XI, sec. 3.

———. 1868. *Acts and Resolutions Chapter 48: An Act to Enable Townships and Incorporated Towns and Cities to Aid in the Construction of Railroads, 27 March 1868.* Des Moines.

Jacklin, Kathleen B. 1958. "Local Aid to Railroads in Illinois, 1848–1870." Master's thesis, Cornell Univ.

Jacobsen, Charles. 1989. "Same Game, Different Players: Problems in Urban Public Utility Regulation, 1850–1987." *Urban Studies* 26: 13–31.

Johns, H. T. 1873. *Duluth.* Duluth, Minn.: n.p.

Johnson, Herbert A., and Ralph K. Andrist. 1977. *Historic Courthouses of New York State: Eighteenth- and Nineteenth-Century Halls of Justice Across the Empire State.* New York: Columbia Univ. Press.

Jones, Robert. 1877. *Tennessee at the Crossroads: The State Debt Controversy, 1870–1883.* Knoxville: Univ. of Tennessee Press.

Josephson, Matthew. 1929. "Detroit: City of Tomorrow, 1929." *Outlook* 151 (Feb. 13, 1929): 243–78. Excerpted in Holli, 162–70.

Karl, Barry D. 1983. *The Uneasy State: The United States from 1915 to 1945.* Chicago: Univ. of Chicago Press.

Kaufman, G. G., and K. T. Rosen, eds. 1981. *The Property Tax Revolt: The Case of Proposition 13.* Cambridge, Mass.: Ballinger.

Keating, J. M. 1886. *History of Memphis.* Syracuse, N.Y.: n.p.

Keller, Morton. 1977. *Affairs of State: Public Life in Late Nineteenth-Century America.* Cambridge, Mass.: Harvard Univ. Press.

Knott, J. Proctor. 1872. *Duluth! Speech of Hon. J. Proctor Knott, of Kentucky, Delivered in the House of Representatives, on the St. Croix and Superior Land Grant, January 27, 1871.* Washington, D.C.: F. & J. Rives & Geo. A. Bailey.

Lebovich, William L. 1984. *America's City Halls.* Washington, D.C.: Preservation Press.

Legler, John B., Richard Sylla, and John J. Wallis. 1986. "United States City Finance and the Growth of Government, 1850–1920." *Journal of Economic History* 48: 347–56.

Leland, Simeon E. 1932. " 'City Broke.' " *Commerce* (Feb.).

Lunt, Richard D. 1965. *The High Ministry of Government: The Political Career of Frank Murphy.* Detroit, Mich.: Wayne State Univ. Press.

McCleary, Richard, Richard A. Hay, Errol E. Meidinger, and David Mc-Dowell. 1980. *Applied Time Series Analysis for the Social Sciences.* Beverly Hills, Calif.: Sage.

McClelland, Peter D., and A. Magdovich. 1981. *Crisis in the Making: The Political Economy of New York State Since 1945.* Cambridge, Eng.: Cambridge Univ. Press.

McClure, Ethel. 1968. *More Than a Roof: The Development of Minnesota Poor Farms and Homes for the Aged.* St. Paul: Minnesota Historical Society.

McCormick, Richard L. 1986. *The Party Period and Public Policy: American Politics from the Age of Jackson to the Progressive Era.* New York: Oxford Univ. Press.

McDonald, Terrence J. 1986. *The Parameters of Urban Fiscal Policy: Socioeconomic Change and Political Culture in San Francisco, 1860–1906.* Berkeley: Univ. of California Press.

———. 1990. "Building the Impossible State: Toward an Institutional Analysis of Statebuilding in America, 1820–1930." In *Institutions in American Society: Essays in Market, Political and Social Organizations,* ed. John E. Jackson, 217–39. Ann Arbor: Univ. of Michigan Press.

McDonald, Terrence J., and Sally Ward, eds., 1984. *The Politics of Urban Fiscal Policy.* Beverly Hills, Calif.: Sage.

McGrane, Reginald C. 1935. *Foreign Bondholders and American State Debts.* New York: Macmillan.

McGrath, C. Peter. 1963. *Morrison R. Waite: The Triumph of Character.* New York: Macmillan.

Merton, R. K. 1949. *Social Theory and Social Structure: Toward the Codification of Theory and Research.* Glencoe, Ill.: Free Press.

Monkkonen, Eric H. 1980. "The Quantitative Historical Study of Crime and Criminal Justice." In *History and Crime: Implications for Criminal Justice Policy,* ed. James A. Inciardi and Charles E. Faupel, 53–73. Beverly Hills, Calif.: Sage.

———. 1981a. "A Disorderly People? Urban Order in Nineteenth- and Twentieth-Century America." *Journal of American History* 68 (Dec.): 539–59.

———. 1981b. *Police in Urban America, 1860–1920.* Cambridge, Eng.: Cambridge Univ. Press.

———. 1981c. "Toward an Understanding of Urbanisation: Drunk Arrests in Los Angeles." *Pacific Historical Review* 50 (May): 234–44.

———. 1982. "From Cop History to Social History: The Significance of the Police in American History," *Journal of Social History* 15 (Summer): 575–91.

———. 1984a. "The Politics of Municipal Indebtedness and Default,

1850–1936." In *The Politics of Urban Fiscal Policy*, ed. Terrence J. Mc-Donald and Sally Ward, 125–59. Beverly Hills, Calif.: Sage.

——, ed. 1984b. *Walking to Work: Tramps in America, 1790–1935*. Lincoln: Univ. of Nebraska Press.

——. 1985. "What Urban Crisis? An Historian's Point of View." *Urban Affairs Quarterly* 20: 429–47.

——. 1988. *America Becomes Urban: The Development of U.S. Cities and Towns, 1780–1980*. Berkeley: Univ. of California Press.

Municipal Corporations — Naval Officers. 1902. Vol. 36 of the *Century Edition of the American Digest*. St. Paul, Minn.: West Publishing.

Newell, Mason H. 1904. "Township Government in Illinois." In *Transactions of the Illinois State Historical Society*, Publication No. 9 of the Illinois State Historical Society Library, 467–94.

Pease, Theodore C., ed. 1925. *The Laws of the Northwest Territory, 1788–1800*. Illinois Historical Collection 17. Springfield, Ill.

Pease, William H., and Jane H. Pease. 1985. *The Web of Progress: Private Values and Public Styles in Boston and Charleston, 1828–1843*. New York: Oxford Univ. Press.

Peet, George, and Gabrielle Keller. 1984. *Courthouses of the Commonwealth.* Amherst: Univ. of Massachusetts Press.

Pegram, Thomas. 1992. *Partisans and Progressives: Private Interest and Public Policy in Illinois, 1870–1922*. Urbana: Univ. of Illinois Press.

Peterson, Paul. 1981. *City Limits*. Chicago: Univ. of Chicago Press.

Pisani, Donald J. 1987. "Promotion and Regulation: Constitutionalism and the American Economy." *Journal of American History* 74: 740–68.

Piven, F. 1977. "The Urban Crisis: Who Got What and Why." In *The Fiscal Crisis of American Cities*, ed. D. Mermelstein and R. E. Alcaly, 132–44.

Piven, F., and R. Cloward. 1971. *Regulating the Poor*. New York: Pantheon Books.

Randall, James G., ed. 1933. *The Diary of Orville Hickman Browning*. Vol. 2, *1865–1881*. Springfield: Illinois State Historical Library.

Ransom, Roger L. 1982. "In Search of Security: The Growth of Government in the United States, 1902–1970." In *Explorations in the New Economic History: Essays in Honor of Douglass C. North*, ed. Roger L. Ransom, Richard Sutch, and Gary M. Walton, 125–47. New York: Academic Press.

Ransom, Roger L., and Richard Sutch. 1977. *One Kind of Freedom: The Economic Consequences of Emancipation*. Cambridge, Eng.: Cambridge Univ. Press.

Redmond, Patrick H. 1869. *History of Quincy and Its Men of Mark*. Quincy, Ill.: Heirs and Russell.

Reed, Robert R. 1912. "Uniform Municipal Bond Legislation." In *Proceedings of the Organization Meeting and of the First Annual Convention of the Investment Banker's Association of America*, ed. Frederick R. Fenton. Chicago: Investment Banker's Association.

Ridley, Clarence, and Orin F. Nolting, eds. 1935. *What the Depression Has Done to Cities*. Chicago: International City Managers' Association.

Rosen, Christine M. 1989. "Smoke Abeyance in Chicago." School of Business, Univ. of California, Berkeley.

Schieber, Harry N. 1982. "The Transportation Revolution and American Law: Constitutionalism and Public Policy." In *Transportation and the Early American Nation*, 1–29. Indianapolis: Indiana Historical Society.

Schulman, Bruce J. 1991. *From Cotton Belt to Sunbelt: Federal Policy, Economic Development, and the Transformation of the South, 1938–1980*. New York: Oxford Univ. Press.

Schultz, C. L., E. R. Fried, A. M. Rivlen, N. H. Teeters, and R. D. Reischaur. 1977. "Fiscal Problems in Cities." In *The Fiscal Crisis of American Cities*, ed. D. Mermelstein and R. E. Alcaly, 189–212.

Schwartz, Gary T. 1973. "The Logic of Home Rule and the Private Law Exception." *UCLA Law Review* (Apr.) 20: 672–777.

Sears, D. O., and J. Citrin. 1982. *Tax Revolt: Something for Nothing in California*. Cambridge, Mass.: Harvard Univ. Press.

Secrist, Henry. 1914. *An Economic Analysis of the Constitutional Restrictions on Public Indebtedness in the United States. Bulletin of the University of Wisconsin #637, Economic and Political Sciences*, vol. 8, no. 1. Madison.

Shade, William G. 1972. *Banks or No Banks: The Money Issue in Western Politics, 1832–1865*. Detroit, Mich.: Wayne State Univ. Press.

Shefter, Martin. 1977. "New York City's Fiscal Crisis." *The Public Interest* 48 (Summer): 98–127.

Shortridge, Ray M. 1981. "Estimating Voter Participation." In *Analyzing Electoral History: A Guide to the Study of American Voting Behavior*, ed. Jerome Clubb, William Flannigan, and Nancy Zingale, 137–52. Beverly Hills, Calif.: Sage.

Siegelman, Peter, and John J. Donohue. 1990. "Studying the Iceberg from Its Tip: A Comparison of Published and Unpublished Employment Discrimination Cases," *Law & Society Review* 24: 1133–70.

Sigafoos, Robert A. 1979. *Cotton Row to Beale Street: A Business History of Memphis*. Memphis, Tenn.: Memphis State Univ. Press.

Skocpol, Theda. 1992. *Protecting Soldiers and Mothers: The Political Origins of Social Policy in the United States*. Cambridge, Mass.: Harvard Univ. Press.

Skowronek, Stephen. 1982. *Building a New American State: The Expansion of National Administrative Capacities, 1877–1920.* Cambridge, Eng.: Cambridge Univ. Press.

Sorrels, William W. 1970. *Memphis' Greatest Debate: A Question of Water.* Memphis, Tenn.: Memphis State Univ. Press.

Steiner, Clyde F., Gilbert Y. Steiner, and Lois Langdon. 1954. *Local Taxing Units: The Illinois Experience.* Urbana, Ill.: Institute of Government and Public Affairs.

Survey of Current Business. 1982. 62 (Aug.): 7.

——. 1983. 63 (Feb.): 5.

Teaford, Jon C. 1975. *The Municipal Revolution in America: Origins of Modern Urban Government, 1650–1825.* Baltimore, Md.: Johns Hopkins Univ. Press.

——. 1979. *City and Suburb: The Political Fragmentation of Metropolitan America, 1850–1970.* Baltimore, Md.: Johns Hopkins Univ. Press.

——. 1984. *The Unheralded Triumph: City Government in America, 1870–1900.* Baltimore, Md.: Johns Hopkins Univ. Press.

Thernstrom, Stephan. 1964. *Progress and Poverty: Social Mobility in a Nineteenth-Century City.* Cambridge, Mass.: Harvard Univ. Press.

——. 1971. "Reflections on the New Urban History." *Dædalus* 100 (Spring): 359–75.

Thernstrom, Stephan, and Richard Sennett. 1969. *Nineteenth-Century Cities.* New Haven, Conn.: Yale Univ. Press.

Tiebout, Charles M. 1956. "A Pure Theory of Local Expenditures." *Journal of Political Economy* 64 (Oct.): 416–24.

Underwood, Kathleen. 1987. *Town Building on the Colorado Frontier.* Albuquerque: Univ. of New Mexico Press.

U.S. Bureau of the Census. 1883. *The Compendium of the Tenth Census, Part I.* Washington, D.C.: USGPO.

U.S. Census Office. 1872a. *Ninth Census of the United States.* Vol. 1, *The Statistics of the Population of the United States.* Washington, D.C.: USGPO.

——. 1872b. *Ninth Census of the United States.* Vol. 3, *The Statistics of the Wealth and Industry of the United States.* Washington, D.C.: USGPO.

——. 1884. *Report on Valuation, Taxation and Public Indebtedness in the United States.* Washington, D.C.: USGPO.

——. 1892. *Report on Wealth, Debt and Taxation.* Part 1, *Public Debt.* Washington, D.C.: USGPO.

U.S. Department of Commerce. Bureau of Economic Analysis. 1981. *The National Income and Product Accounts of the United States, 1929–76: A Supplement to the Survey of Current Business.* Washington, D.C.: USGPO.

Van de Woestyne, Royal S. 1935. *State Control of Local Finance in Massachusetts*. Cambridge, Mass.: Harvard Univ. Press.

Virtue, Maxine. 1949. "The Public Use of Private Capital: A Discussion of Problems Related to Municipal Bond Financing." *Virginia Law Review* 35: 285–315.

Wade, Richard W. 1979. "America's Cities Are (Mostly) Better Than Ever." *American Heritage* 30 (Feb.–Mar.): 6–13.

Ward, David. 1964. "A Comparative Historiographical Geography of Streetcar Suburbs in Boston, Massachusetts, and Leeds, England, 1850–1920." *Annals of the Association of American Geographers* 54: 477–89.

Warren, Charles. 1935. *The Supreme Court in United States History*. Vol. 2. Boston: Little, Brown.

Wengert, Egbert S. *Financial Problems of the City of Detroit in the Depression*. Detroit, Mich.: Bureau of Governmental Research.

Whyte, William F. 1916. "The Watertown Railway Bond Fight." In *Proceedings of the Wisconsin State Historical Society*, 268–307. Madison: State Historical Society of Wisconsin.

Williams, C. Dickerman, and Peter R. Nehemkis, Jr. 1937. "Municipal Improvements as Affected by Constitutional Debt Limitations." *Columbia Law Review* 37: 177–211.

Woodbridge, David A., and John S. Pardee. 1910. *History of Duluth and St. Louis County*. 2 vols. Chicago: C. F. Cooper.

Yearly, Clifton K. 1970. *The Money Machines: The Breakdown and Reform of Governmental and Party Finance in the North, 1860–1920*. Albany: State Univ. of New York Press.

Young, Robert A. 1991. "Planning via Redevelopment: The Orange County Municipal Experience." *Journal of Orange County Studies* 5/6: 18–29.

Zunz, Olivier. 1982. *The Changing Face of Inequality: Urbanization, Industrial Development, and Immigrants in Detroit, 1880–1920*. Chicago: Univ. of Chicago Press.

Index

In this index an "f" after a number indicates a separate reference on the next page, and an "ff" indicates separate references on the next two pages. A continuous discussion over two or more pages is indicated by a span of page numbers, e.g., "57–59." *Passim* is used for a cluster of references in close but not consecutive sequence.

Library of Congress
Cataloging-in-Publication

Monkkonen, Eric H.
    The local state : public money and American cities / Eric H.
Monkkonen.
    p.   cm. — (Stanford studies in the new political history)
Includes bibliographical references and index.
ISBN 0-8047-2412-1 (cloth)
    1. Municipal finance — United States.   2. Municipal finance —
Illinois.   3. Fiscal policy — United States.   4. Fiscal policy —
Illinois.   I. Title.   II. Series.
HJ9145.M66   1995
336'.01473 — dc20   95-1074   CIP

⊗ This book is printed on acid-free, recycled paper.

Original printing 1995

Last figure below indicates year of this printing:

04 03 02 01 00 99 98 97 96 95